CAMPAIGN 380

NARVIK 1940

The Battle for Northern Norway

DAVID GREENTREE   ILLUSTRATED BY RAMIRO BUJEIRO

Series editor Nikolai Bogdanovic

OSPREY PUBLISHING
Bloomsbury Publishing Plc
Kemp House, Chawley Park, Cumnor Hill, Oxford OX2 9PH, UK
29 Earlsfort Terrace, Dublin 2, Ireland
1385 Broadway, 5th Floor, New York, NY 10018, USA
E-mail: info@ospreypublishing.com
www.ospreypublishing.com

OSPREY is a trademark of Osprey Publishing Ltd

First published in Great Britain in 2022

© Osprey Publishing Ltd, 2022

A catalogue record for this book is available from the British Library.

ISBN: PB 9781472849106; eBook 9781472849113; ePDF 9781472849083;
XML 9781472849090

22 23 24 25 26   10 9 8 7 6 5 4 3 2 1

Maps by Bounford.com
3D BEVs by Paul Kime
Index by Alison Worthington
Typeset by PDQ Digital Media Solutions, Bungay, UK
Printed and bound in India by Replika Press Private Ltd.

FSC
MIX
Paper from
responsible sources
FSC® C016779
www.fsc.org

Artist's note

Readers may care to note that the original paintings from which the colour
plates in this book were prepared are available for private sale. All
reproduction copyright whatsoever is retained by the publishers. The artist
can be contacted at the following email address:

ramirobujeiro@yahoo.com.ar

The publishers regret that they can enter into no correspondence upon
this matter.

Osprey Publishing supports the Woodland Trust, the UK's leading woodland
conservation charity.

To find out more about our authors and books visit
www.ospreypublishing.com. Here you will find extracts, author
interviews, details of forthcoming events and the option to sign up for
our newsletter.

Acknowledgements

I would like to thank my uncle Colin Greentree for helping with the
translation of German primary sources. Aasta Karlsen from the inter-
municipal archive located at Bodø facilitated use of the many different
sources from the Dag Skogheim collection. Photos from this collection are
used throughout this book. Thanks again to the series editor, Nikolai
Bogdanovic, for his patience and guidance.

Acronyms and abbreviations

ADC	aide de camp
ASDIC	Anti-Submarine Detection Investigation Committee
ATR	anti-tank rifle
CQSM	Company Quartermaster Sergeant-Major
CSM	Company Sergeant-Major
GHQ	general headquarters
HA	heavy artillery
HE	high-explosive
HMG	heavy machine gun
HQ	headquarters
LCA	landing craft (assault)
LCM	landing craft (mechanized)
LMG	light machine gun
MC	Military Cross
MG	machine gun
MMG	medium machine gun
NM	nautical miles
OP	observation post
RSM	Regimental Sergeant-Major
SMG	sub machine gun

Unit identification

Battalions are identified with Roman numerals followed by point and forward
slash before the regiment name: e.g. III./Gebirgsjäger-Regiment 139.
Companies are identified with Arabic numerals followed by point and
forward slash before the regiment name: e.g. 2./Gebirgsjäger-Regiment 139.

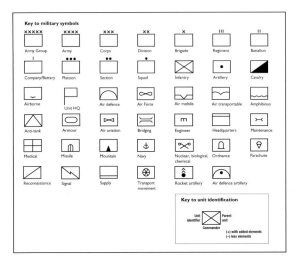

Front cover main illustration: Norwegian troops from 2nd Platoon, 2nd
Company, Trønder Battalion commanded by Lieutenant Helge Brinchmann
withdraw from Moan as Gebirgsjägers launch their attack on 25 April 1940.
(Ramiro Bujeiro)
Title page photograph: Troops of 6./Gebirgsjäger-Regiment 137 lead the
pursuit of Allied forces on 4 May 1940, hauling their equipment in carts.
(Arkiv i Nordland, CC BY-SA 2.0)

CONTENTS

ORIGINS OF THE CAMPAIGN

On the afternoon of 6 April, Gebirgsjäger-Regiment 139 with the staff of 3.Gebirgs-Division, commanded by Generalleutnant Dietl, travelled to Bremerhaven and then on to Wesermünde on the North Sea coast where they boarded ten destroyers. Most of the men had never been to sea before and the rank and file knew nothing of where they were going or why. Once they had left port at 2300hrs, they were told the destination of the convoy: Narvik, the Norwegian iron ore town north of the Arctic Circle, 1,200NM distant. The landing needed to take place on 9 April at 0500hrs precisely.

The battleships *Gneisenau* and *Scharnhorst* joined the destroyers of *Gruppe Narvik* early the next morning. Also joining them on part of the journey was the contingent destined for Trondheim with most of Gebirgsjäger-Regiment 138, escorted by the heavy cruiser *Admiral Hipper* and four destroyers. Spotted by British planes that morning, Allied bombers attacked them in the afternoon, causing no damage. German signals intelligence reported that the British had ordered cruisers and destroyers to intercept them. The fleet headed on through the rainy darkness, past the Shetlands, pushed on by Force 8 winds, the ships keeping some distance from each other in order not to collide.

By the morning of 8 April, the fleet was off Trondheim, slowing to allow stragglers to close. The ships pitched up to 50 degrees and steering was difficult. Speeds needed to be slower, as the wind was pushing them from the stern. Munitions crates were swept overboard. Seasickness was rife. At 0802hrs, the British destroyer *Glowworm* appeared. Only with the help of *Admiral Hipper* was *Glowworm* set on fire and sunk. *Gruppe Trondheim* then departed the fleet. The weather was still foul. In the early afternoon, a German Do 26 aircraft detected the British Home Fleet sailing near the Orkneys, approaching Gruppe Narvik. German radar detected ships 190NM distant. The German battleships managed to escort the destroyers to Vestfjord and then at 2100hrs sailed to engage the British fleet.

The German destroyers, meanwhile, had to plough on through Force 10 winds. The streamlined shape of the ships did not help and turbulent seas threw them from side to side. The change in wind direction did enable them to maintain a good pace, despite the difficulties, thus reducing the consumption of limited fuel stocks. The storm had led the British to send the Home Fleet out to sea, except for the British 2nd Destroyer Flotilla that sought the protection of the Lofoten Islands near the entrance to

Northern Norway, 9 April–8 June 1940

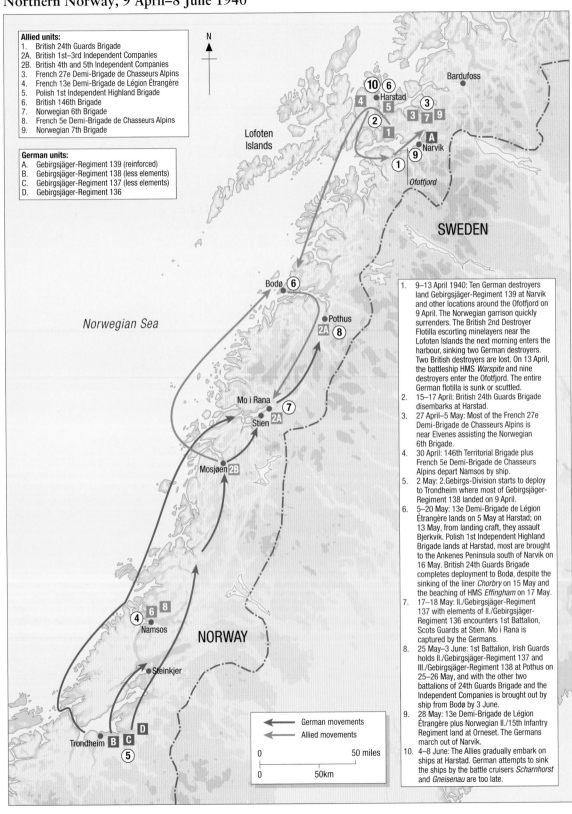

Allied units:
1. British 24th Guards Brigade
2A. British 1st–3rd Independent Companies
2B. British 4th and 5th Independent Companies
3. French 27e Demi-Brigade de Chasseurs Alpins
4. French 13e Demi-Brigade de Légion Étrangère
5. Polish 1st Independent Highland Brigade
6. British 146th Brigade
7. Norwegian 6th Brigade
8. French 5e Demi-Brigade de Chasseurs Alpins
9. Norwegian 7th Brigade

German units:
A. Gebirgsjäger-Regiment 139 (reinforced)
B. Gebirgsjäger-Regiment 138 (less elements)
C. Gebirgsjäger-Regiment 137 (less elements)
D. Gebirgsjäger-Regiment 136

Bardufoss

Harstad

Narvik

Ofotfjord

SWEDEN

Lofoten Islands

Norwegian Sea

Bodø

Pothus

Mo i Rana

Stien

Mosjøen

Namsos

NORWAY

Steinkjer

Trondheim

← German movements
← Allied movements

0 _____ 50 miles

0 _____ 50km

1. 9–13 April 1940: Ten German destroyers land Gebirgsjäger-Regiment 139 at Narvik and other locations around the Ofotfjord on 9 April. The Norwegian garrison quickly surrenders. The British 2nd Destroyer Flotilla escorting minelayers near the Lofoten Islands the next morning enters the harbour, sinking two German destroyers. Two British destroyers are lost. On 13 April, the battleship HMS *Warspite* and nine destroyers enter the Ofotfjord. The entire German flotilla is sunk or scuttled.

2. 15–17 April: British 24th Guards Brigade disembarks at Harstad.

3. 27 April–5 May: Most of the French 27e Demi-Brigade de Chasseurs Alpins is near Elvenes assisting the Norwegian 6th Brigade.

4. 30 April: 146th Territorial Brigade plus French 5e Demi-Brigade de Chasseurs Alpins depart Namsos by ship.

5. 2 May: 2.Gebirgs-Division starts to deploy to Trondheim where most of Gebirgsjäger-Regiment 138 landed on 9 April.

6. 5–20 May: 13e Demi-Brigade de Légion Étrangère lands on 5 May at Harstad; on 13 May, from landing craft, they assault Bjerkvik. Polish 1st Independent Highland Brigade lands at Harstad, most are brought to the Ankenes Peninsula south of Narvik on 16 May. British 24th Guards Brigade completes deployment to Bodø, despite the sinking of the liner *Chorbry* on 15 May and the beaching of HMS *Effingham* on 17 May.

7. 17–18 May: II./Gebirgsjäger-Regiment 137 with elements of II./Gebirgsjäger-Regiment 136 encounters 1st Battalion, Scots Guards at Stien. Mo i Rana is captured by the Germans.

8. 25 May–3 June: 1st Battalion, Irish Guards holds II./Gebirgsjäger-Regiment 137 and III./Gebirgsjäger-Regiment 138 at Pothus on 25–26 May, and with the other two battalions of 24th Guards Brigade and the Independent Companies is brought out by ship from Bodø by 3 June.

9. 28 May: 13e Demi-Brigade de Légion Étrangère plus Norwegian II./15th Infantry Regiment land at Orneset. The Germans march out of Narvik.

10. 4–8 June: The Allies gradually embark on ships at Harstad. German attempts to sink the ships by the battle cruisers *Scharnhorst* and *Gneisenau* are too late.

Vestfjord. Near midnight, the storm abated and in the shelter of the islands sea conditions improved considerably. At 0300hrs on 9 April, the German destroyers entered Ofotfjord. Norwegian patrol ships detected them and reported to higher authority. Dramatic white peaks rising to 1,000m greeted the Germans as they approached the narrows between Hamnes and Ramnes, the supposed location of Norwegian coastal batteries, each ship following the wake of the ship in front. Two destroyers, each offloading a company from Gebirgsjäger-Regiment 139, were detailed to land at the promontories to assault the batteries. By 0700hrs, both companies (1. and 6./Gebirgsjäger-Regiment 139), struggling through deep snow, had reported that the battery positions 100m up the slopes did not possess any guns and then the soldiers re-embarked. If the guns did exist and were captured they would have had a significant effect on British entry through the straits. Three destroyers had, meanwhile, proceeded to the entrance of Narvik harbour while three others had proceeded up Herjangsfjord to land soldiers at the Norwegian army depot there.

The importance of Swedish iron ore had determined Germany's decision to land soldiers on Norwegian territory. Nearly 45 per cent of the iron ore that Germany imported in 1938 was from Sweden. During the summer months, the Swedish ports could be used; these froze over in winter when trains took the iron ore to the ice-free harbour in Narvik, in Norway to be loaded onto ships that brought it to Germany. Demands for iron ore would substantially increase once the economy was on a war footing. German High Command was worried that the Allies might seize the port to deny Germany this supply. Admiral Raeder, the chief of the naval staff, wrote of how he was convinced that the Allies would occupy Narvik and may move onto the Swedish iron ore mines at Gällivare. He also wanted to use the German fleet to lay siege to Britain. The head of the U-boat arm, Konteradmiral Dönitz, had told Raeder that Trondheim would make a useful U-boat base. Then the Abwehr supplied intelligence of a British cabinet meeting on 19 September 1939 that discussed military intervention to secure the ore railway.

The German notion of occupying Norway was something that had been considered during World War I. The Allied blockade of Germany could be broken if Norway was occupied. Then a German blockade of Britain could be attempted. The army was not keen and the plans were shelved. Despite this, throughout the 1930s Vice-Admiral Wegener continued to suggest that the occupation of Norway would allow the German fleet freedom of the seas, something its geographical position had denied Germany. Raeder did not necessarily agree with Wegener's arguments and placed greater emphasis on guaranteeing the Swedish iron ore supply. When Norway showed it was not willing to stop British ships from cruising within Norwegian territorial waters, the ability to stop the Allies from landing on its shores was questioned by the German leadership, as was the intention of the British to respect Norwegian neutrality.

CHRONOLOGY

1940

5 February   Germany assembles a planning group for the invasion of Norway. The Allied Supreme War Council agrees to occupy Narvik with the occupation of the Swedish ore mines along the railway as the primary strategic aim.

1 March   Germany issues the operational directive Operation *Weserübung*.

2 April   Hitler orders the invasion of Norway. The naval forces will depart at different times to ensure landings will all occur early on 9 April.

5 April   Operation *Wilfrid*, the British mine-laying operation to prevent iron ore ships sailing from Narvik, begins.

7 April   Ten destroyers carrying 2,000 soldiers from Gebirgsjäger-Regiment 139 with Generalleutnant Dietl commanding depart German ports and head for Narvik.

8 April   Captain Warburton-Lee's British 2nd Destroyer Squadron is ordered out of Vestfjord on completion of mine-laying operations as storms threaten the ships. This allows the German destroyers to enter the fjord.

9 April   German destroyers land soldiers at Narvik and other locations by Ofotfjord. The Norwegian garrison commander surrenders.

10 April   Warburton-Lee enters Ofotfjord and surprises German destroyers anchored by the town, sinking two. He also loses two destroyers when other German destroyers ambush him from side fjords.

13 April   The battleship *Warspite* and nine destroyers enter Ofotfjord and eight German destroyers either scuttle or are sunk.

15–17 April   The British 24th (Guards) Brigade lands at Harstad.

25 April   The Norwegian Trønder Battalion is ambushed by elements of Major Stautner's III./Gebirgsjäger-Regiment 139 at Gratangen, losing 275 men.

27 April   The French 27e Demi-Brigade de Chasseurs Alpins start landing near Elvenes.

5 May   French 13e Demi-Brigade de Légion Étrangère lands at Harstad.

7–8 May   The Polish Independent Highland Brigade lands at Harstad.

13 May   French 13e Demi-Brigade de Légion Étrangère uses landing craft to assault Bjerkvik.

15 May	The Irish Guards on board *Chorbry*, hit by a bomb from a German aircraft late on 14 May, are brought off by destroyers and go back to Harstad. They were heading for Bodø.
16 May	Polish forces are brought to the Ankenes Peninsula where they replace British and French forces.
17 May	The British South Wales Borderers on board *Effingham* are brought off when the ship runs aground. The battalion also heading for Bodø is brought to Harstad.

The Scots Guards defend the position at Stien from II./Gebirgsjäger-Regiment 137 marching from Finneid. The Germans are part of a larger force from 2.Gebirgs-Division sent to Trondheim to march on Narvik and join Dietl's Gebirgsjäger-Regiment 139. |
| 18 May | The Scots Guards withdraw through Mo.

The Polish attacks on the Ankenes Peninsula do not succeed. |
| 23 May | Supported by elements from Independent Companies, the Scots Guards occupy positions at Storfjord on the other side of the snow plateau.

The Irish Guards landed at Bodø on 20 May go to Pothus where they establish defence positions with British No. 2 and No. 3 Independent companies and Norwegian elements on 24 May. |
25–26 May	II./Gebirgsjäger-Regiment 137 is held by the Irish Guards at Pothus. The Pothus position is abandoned on 26 May when the Irish Guards withdraw to Saltfjord.
28 May	The French Légion Étrangère and Norwegian forces from Øyjord land at Orneset. The Poles attack the Ankenes Peninsula. Both operations are successful. The Germans withdraw from Narvik and establish a new line on the railway and on heights at the end of Beisfjord.
31 May	The Norwegians attack German defenders on hill 620 near the Swedish border. A small German force stops them only temporarily; when they run out of ammunition the Germans abandon the position.
1–3 June	British forces embark on ships at Bodø and most sail to Harstad.
4–8 June	The Allies gradually embark on ships at Harstad and head for Scapa Flow. Narvik is abandoned, the Germans are slow to realize this is occurring and do not interdict the withdrawal.
8 June	*Scharnhorst* and *Gneisenau*, at sea since 4 June, do not know the withdrawal is happening. They are tasked with attacking ships and bases near the Harstad area. They are told of the presence of a convoy, though they are too late to intercept it. They do happen upon the aircraft carrier *Glorious* and sink the ship.

OPPOSING COMMANDERS

ALLIED

British

Admiral of the Fleet William Boyle, Earl of Cork and Orrey was the commander of the Anglo-French expedition that was preparing to assist the Finns. When this was abandoned he was appointed the commander of the naval force of the Narvik expedition. He would not meet his army counterpart until they had landed and did not get on with him personally or professionally.

Born in 1873, Cork was a junior officer on the China Station during the Boxer Rebellion. He was a staff officer during the Dardanelles Campaign of 1915 and then Red Sea patrol commander from 1916. He was appointed captain of his first battlecruiser, HMS *Tiger*, in 1919. By 1932 he was promoted admiral, commanding the Home Fleet the following year. He went on to command the Portsmouth base and was Admiral of the Fleet by the start of World War II.

He initially wanted to land men at Narvik as quick as possible. However, Major-General Pierse Mackesy discouraged him from doing so. When Cork was elevated to commander of the expedition from commander of the fleet at Narvik, he agreed with Mackesy not to land forces near Narvik without first occupying the Beisfjord and Rombaksfjord high ground. He landed the French Légion Étrangère at Bjerkvik for them to approach Rombaksfjord and only then launched a combined French and Norwegian force on the Framnes Peninsula to capture Narvik. By then a withdrawal from Norway was being planned. The Germans needed to be thrown out of the town to ensure the evacuation would not be seen by the land forces. This would be his last command appointment.

Major-General Pierse Mackesy was born on 5 April 1883 and commissioned a second lieutenant with the Royal Engineers aged 19. Promoted to captain by 1916 to command an engineer company, from 1917 to 1918 he was on the Western Front. During the Russian Civil War, he was a staff officer serving with the forces helping the Whites. By 1935, there followed command of a brigade and by 1938 he was commanding a division. Mackesy's British 49th (West Riding) Division was destined for France when news of the expedition to Norway was passed to him. His experience of Arctic conditions, because of service during the Russian Civil War, made him a natural choice to command an expedition to Narvik. However, he would not command his own brigades; these would be sent to conduct a pincer movement on Trondheim. Instead, he would command the British 24th (Guards) Brigade. He deemed this force insufficient to launch a direct landing on the town and consistently stated such an operation would be a disaster. He was sent home while the attack on Bjerkvik was being launched. He would not be appointed to another command.

Major-General Carl Gustav Fleischer was the commander of the Norwegian 6th Division. He was born in 1883, commissioned an officer aged 22 and he was a captain by 1917. Fleischer was a teacher at the Norwegian Defence College from 1928 to 1934. He wrote profusely about the best ways to defend Norway, suggesting a combination of holding onto coastal positions while at the same time mobilizing from the protection of the interior. By 1930 he was a major and by 1934 he commanded the Norwegian 14th Infantry Regiment at Mosjøen as a colonel. With the Winter War erupting by late 1939, he mobilized his Norwegian 6th Division and encouraged increased

Major-General Carl Gustav Fleischer. (Matteo Omied/Alamy)

military readiness to keep out Russian forces. He would not rely on Allied forces, suggested by the head of the Norwegian Army, Major-General Ruge, and would steadfastly try to destroy the German contingent around Narvik. While the French and Polish concentrated on Narvik, for the most part Norwegian forces attempted to go around German positions and block the railway from Sweden. On 7 June, when the Allies decided to withdraw, he was made commander of the exiled Norwegian Army, though most formations were not brought out by the Allied ships. He would encourage commando raids on the Norwegian coast and was bypassed when the post of commander of all Norwegian Armed Forces went to a young major. Humiliated, he shot himself with his pistol on 19 December 1942.

Major-General Colin Gubbins was commissioned by the start of World War I aged 18. He was a gunner and on 22 May 1915 first saw service at the Second Battle of Ypres. He was at the Battle of the Somme and won the MC for rescuing wounded men while being shot at. By early 1918, Captain Gubbins was at the Battle of St Quentin. By April he was suffering from trench fever and was out of the line. In 1919 he was General Ironside's ADC during the North Russia Campaign against the Bolsheviks. He was also an intelligence officer during the Anglo-Irish War. Gubbins was with signals intelligence at GHQ India, and then graduated from the Staff College at Quetta. In 1931, he joined the Russian section of the War Office. Promoted to lieutenant-colonel by early April 1939, he wrote training manuals on tactics for resistance movements. He also discussed sabotage operations with the Polish General Staff and was Chief of Staff to the military mission sent to Warsaw. By October he was in Paris as head of the military mission helping Czech and Polish forces.

He was summoned from France early in 1940 to raise the Independent Companies, the forerunners of the British Commandos. Five would be sent to Norway and Gubbins assumed command of the British 24th (Guards) Brigade at Bodø. He would dismiss Lieutenant-Colonel Trappes-Lomax

Generalleutnant Eduard Dietl, in a portrait taken in 1943. (INTERFOTO/Alamy)

for disobeying orders. Once back in Britain, he was tasked with forming the Auxiliary Units, a commando force based on the Home Guard, which would conduct sabotage operations if the Germans landed. By late 1940, he was with SOE (Special Operations Executive), established to co-ordinate sabotage within enemy-occupied territory. By September 1943 he was leading that organization. When SOE was disbanded in 1946, the War Office had no further use for him.

GERMAN

Generalleutnant Eduard Dietl joined the army on 1 October 1909 and fought on the Western Front throughout World War I, rising to company commander and *Oberleutnant*. He was a committed Nazi in the post-war period, and throughout the 1920s and 30s he continued to be promoted. He was an *Oberstleutant* by the time of the Nazi seizure of power in 1933 and by the start of World War II he was a *Generalmajor*. Promoted *Generalleutnant* immediately before the expedition to Narvik, he would lead 3.Gebirgs-Division elements based on Gebirgsjäger-Regiment 139 throughout the battle. His situation was difficult, with Allied soldiers soon outnumbering his force. His men experienced inhospitable conditions; Dietl made sure he would share the fate of his men. His other regiment, Gebirgsjäger-Regiment 138, was landed at Trondheim and, supported by elements of 2.Gebirgs-Division, would attempt to get to him while he was still holding out. He was awarded the *Ritterkreuz* on 9 May and the Oak Leaves on 19 June. The following month he was made *General der Gebirgstruppe* and commanded Gebirgs-Korps Norwegen, comprising 2.Gebirgs-Division and 3.Gebirgs-Division. He was promoted *Generaloberst* and took command of 20.Gebirgs-Armee, fighting to capture Murmansk, in northern Russia, and guard the nikel mines near Petsamo. On 23 June 1944 the aircraft with Dietl on board crashed and he was killed. From a modest social background, he was popular with his men and his Finnish Allies. Goebbels, the propaganda minister, made sure he was seen to be a national hero.

Major Ludwig Stautner, commander of I./Gebirgsjäger-Regiment 139, was born on 4 May 1895. During World War I, he was decorated with the Golden Bavarian Order of Merit after he stormed a French position in September 1916, eliminating an MG. He was a junior NCO with Jäger-Bataillon 6 during this operation, and he would be commissioned *Leutnant der Reserve* in early 1918. He was a battalion commander by 1939, taking his battalion to fight in the Polish campaign. He was awarded the *Ritterkreuz* on 20 June 1940 for the attack he launched on Norwegian soldiers occupying a camp near Elvenes, following a personal reconnaissance. The attack started during the hours of darkness nearly destroyed the Norwegian Trønder Battalion. He would be promoted *Oberst* and commanded Gebirgsjäger-Regiment 139 while fighting as part of 20.*Gebirgs-Armee*. He survived the war.

OPPOSING FORCES

ALLIED

Norwegian

Following World War I, the Norwegians decided to look into how the size of the army could be reduced. From 1930, the politicians not the military were responsible for the state of the Armed Forces. The Norwegian Labour Party wanted to disarm the military and replace it with a police force. When it formed the government from 1935 disarmament was no longer possible, because of the international situation, and if the Labour Party was to stay in government, it had to change its policy. Still, the reductions in military spending throughout the 1920s had degraded the army's capabilities. Training set at 144 days for conscripts immediately following World War I was only 60 days for infantry by 1935 and the number of officers was reduced by 60 per cent. Equipment was not modernized and the 1894 Krag–Jørgensen rifle was still being used. The 6.5mm Madsen was the LMG. The HMG was the M29 Colt. Increases in defence spending, once the threat of war was apparent by the late 1930s, were not enough. The Labour Party persisted with the opinion that the army could launch a military coup. Quisling's Party of National Unity was not a political force to be reckoned with, although perhaps 20 per cent of the junior officer cadre were members. Following the fall of Norway, 1,150 Norwegian officers decided to join or renew their membership of the Party of National Unity.

Norwegian recruits from the Norwegian Trønder Battalion, 12th Infantry Regiment are seen here near the Soviet border in 1940. Fleischer, with his 6th District HQ at Tromsø, if able to fully mobilize, had Norwegian 14th Infantry Regiment at Mosjøen, Norwegian 15th Infantry Regiment at Elvegårdsmoen near Narvik, and Norwegian 16th Infantry Regiment at Tromsø and Bardufoss. On 8 April, he had two groups commanded by colonels Fay and Loken. These groups comprised, along with 6th District formation, regiments of other districts on Neutrality Watch. (Municipal Archives of Trondheim, CC BY-SA 2.0)

On 8 April, the army was only partially mobilized with 13,000 out of 90,000 men mobilized, excluding border militia. Six military districts existed with each possessing a divisional HQ. Districts could theoretically mobilize six battalions. Most formations would be slow to mobilize, except for Fleischer's 6th District. Ruge had argued that if neutrality was Norwegian foreign policy, the quicker the army could mobilize the sooner the policy could be implemented. However, a lack of

The winter campaigning made the use of camouflage smocks essential, as demonstrated by these relaxed soldiers from the Norwegian Trønder Battalion, 12th Infantry Regiment. While officers were professional soldiers, the enlisted men comprised conscripts called up for limited training. (Municipal Archives of Trondheim, CC BY-SA 2.0)

funds had led to his ideas going nowhere. At the other five HQs, the Neutrality Watch did permit single battalions to gather to be trained. Some battalions were already on Neutrality Watch to assist 6th Brigade.

The battalion's three companies, each of four platoons, had primarily to use the rifle and LMG. Each platoon had two officers/ NCOs plus 36 men with two LMGs, though some had more, perhaps purloined from the depot. The company had two trucks and six wagons. No grenades or SMGs were issued. The battalion's MG Company had three platoons each with three HMGs. Each platoon had three officers/NCOs with another three with the staff and quartermaster platoons. The battalion also had a staff company made up of four platoons: communications, mortar, medical and quartermaster, as well as a small battalion staff. At full strength, there were 850 men. However, ammunition stocks were inadequate, based on only ten days of combat. The battalion commander had at his direct disposal two 81mm m/34 mortars of Brandt-Stokes design. With limited training on mortars and HMGs, sometimes officers had to fire them. A brigade had a reconnaissance company with two cycle platoons each of four sections. Again, only two LMGs were allocated per platoon. Pioneer platoons had explosives for demolition work, though no land mines. They did important work setting up roadblocks.

Fleischer with formations from other districts had two brigade-sized groups mobilized, commanded by colonels Faye and Loken. Colonel Faye with Norwegian I./12th Infantry Regiment, Norwegian II./14th Infantry Regiment, a motorized artillery battery and platoon elements of divisional support units was based around Finnmark. Norwegian I./12th Infantry Regiment would be brought south from Finnmark by 20 April. Norwegian I./14th Infantry Regiment and the reserve battalion were mobilizing at Mosjøen.

Colonel Loken at Tromsø commanded Norwegian II./15th Infantry Regiment at Setermoen. The battalion was ordered to the Elvegårdsmoen depot on 8 April. They were preparing for demobilization, as they had just done two months on Neutrality Watch. Norwegian I./15th Infantry

Many Norwegian battalions engaged at Narvik had recently done Neutrality Watch and were fit soldiers; however, during this time training was limited, because the poor weather meant that clearing roads and building shelters was the primary role. Some had had compulsory training during the previous six years. Many sent to the border areas, such as this patrol from the Norwegian Trønder Battalion, did ski, unlike some others from coastal communities mobilized later on. (Municipal Archives of Trondheim, CC BY-SA 2.0)

Regiment was only mobilized by May, because the depot had been lost to the Germans. The reserve battalion was not formed. Loken also commanded Norwegian I./16th Infantry Regiment, which mobilized by 13 April at Setermoen near Tromsø. Norwegian II./16th Infantry Regiment and the reserve battalion mobilized at Setermoen in April. However, these men had not done time on the border and the training they had done had happened during the summer months. The soldiers needed skiing practice, because many had not skied for years. Many of them were fishermen and small holders. Norwegian II./16th Infantry Regiment would be sent to the front on 24 April. The 15km road march to positions at Salangen would be challenging. The soldiers were aghast that they would be sleeping outside in tents. The local defence battalion would not be used on the frontline. The Norwegian 6th District support companies were located at Tromsø, as was the NCO school.

A Norwegian Army 7.5cm field gun m/01 and crew during the fighting north of Narvik, May 1940. Each Norwegian district either had a gun regiment of eight 75mm m/01 guns and eight 120mm m/32 howitzers or a mountain regiment of between eight to 12 75mm m/19 guns. The artillery battalion had a communications platoon and an MG platoon. Norwegian 3rd Mountain Artillery Battalion with three batteries (one was motorized and was sent to Øyjord on 8 April) was near Tromsø. Some regiments would place guns on requisitioned trucks, as they could not be towed because of the wooden spoke wheels. (Matteo Omied/Alamy)

Located at the Elvegårdsmoen depot to demobilize, Norwegian I./13th Infantry Regiment, minus a company, was the nearest battalion to Narvik. The other company was by the harbour with 6th Pioneer Company, 6th Machine Gun Battery and a 40mm Bofors battery. The depot of the Norwegian 13th Infantry Regiment was at Steinkjer; 2nd Battalion had just set up there to replace 1st Battalion. A local defence infantry battalion was also established. These forces would be used to slow German forces attacking north out of Trondheim.

British

When World War II broke out, the Irish Guards were at Wellington barracks in London. On 4 October 1939, a month into the war, the Irish Guards took over Public Duties from the Scots Guards, and were told to protect the palaces if bombs struck. Officers were sent on specialist training courses and reservists were called up.

A two-week company training course was completed at Woking by two companies of Irish Guards during that October. A sniper's course at Bisley in Surrey was attended by two sections of men. Yet on 20 December I./Irish Guards was still holding inter-company drill competitions. In January 1940 a 2in mortar course was held when sights finally arrived. All officers were told how they worked.

The 24th (Guards) Brigade was formed on 13 February 1940. I./Irish Guards packed ready to move on 13 March and on 15 March they unpacked for the second time. Extra Bren guns were issued, one to each section, and each platoon was issued the Boys ATR. A ceremonial march on St Patrick's Day through London took place on 17 March. On 5 April they were told to pack; this was the fourth warning of an impending move.

However, the British training regime was no match for that received by the Gebirgsjäger. The equipment did not compare either. The Bren gun, the

A Scots Guards Bren gun team and rifleman in training on Salisbury Plain, 1939. At several points during February and March 1940, prior to embarking for Norway, companies of the Irish Guards conducted shooting and mortar practice at the Ranges Camp, Pirbright, 30 miles west of London. (© Imperial War Museum, H 378)

section LMG, was built for accuracy, not rate of fire. The 30-round magazines it used were designed for small bursts of fire and to hit a target successfully. The belt-fed German MG 34 was able to sustain its fire and deny the enemy the ability to move. British doctrine stipulated that small independent units deploying on operations throughout the Empire must keep the peace. In wartime, formations that operated with limited logistics and large amounts of ammunition did not suit this practice.

Infantry battalions comprised an HQ company and four rifle companies. The HQ company had six platoons, including a mortar, carrier, pioneer and signals platoon. The rifle companies had three platoons each. The mortar platoon only had two 3in mortars with two trucks, and the range of the mortar was only 1,600 yards. Signals platoons relied on cable to enable the battalion commander to communicate with his companies and the carrier and mortar platoons on the phone. Orderlies could also pass messages and these personnel were designated by the company commanders. The admin platoon dealt with the carriage of ammunition and supplies by 30cwt trucks. A platoon of four sections, each with a Boys ATR and Bren gun, was with HQ company to guard against enemy planes. The carrier platoon used the Bren gun carrier, fully tracked and open topped, with light armour on all sides, offering some protection from small arms; and it was capable of motoring at 30mph. A Bren gun or Boys ATR could be operated from the front by the commander through a small aperture. The idea was that the commander and gunner would unload with the Bren or ATR and help the infantry to attack. The pioneer platoon was a large section of tradesmen with a truck.

The infantry platoons had three sections of eight men issued with the bolt-action Lee-Enfield rifle with a ten-round magazine. The Bren gun, crewed by a gunner and his assistant, was the most important section weapon. The platoon HQ had a 2in mortar with a range of 500m and was principally a weapon used to fire smoke rounds. HE could also be used. The Boys ATR with the platoon HQ used a 0.55in round and each magazine had five rounds. The platoon also had a 15cwt truck. Company HQ comprised a major and captain with ten men. A CSM and CQSM assisted the officers as did the clerk, two batmen, a store man and three orderlies. Two trucks were also attached to company HQ.

The Independent Companies were formed from 20 to 22 April to carry out raids from the sea. They each comprised 289 officers and men, and Lieutenant-Colonel Gubbins, who had written draft proposals about these formations operating independently, commanded them. Raised from volunteers from the first and second line TA formations, each TA division formed a company, each brigade forming a platoon. The high percentage of officers permitted some second lieutenants to command sections. A ship would be assigned to each company to be a floating base with supplies on board.

Major Hugh Stockwell, who had put his name forward to command No. 2 Independent Company, was chosen on 22 April. The men started to arrive the next day, although most did not arrive until 25 April. A support section was formed along with the three platoons. The company had 15 infantry officers. Unfortunately, 56 men had to be sent back, because they did not pass medical inspection. Only 32 replacements were chosen by the battalions; battalion commanders said they could opt out, but most did not.

On 1 May, Stockwell was told about the type of irregular warfare his company was expected to carry out. When he returned to his unit, he put the company through rigorous physical and tactical exercises on rough terrain. A sniper rifle and two Thompson SMGs were issued per section. Each section also had a Bren gun. The platoon HQ had two Boys ATRs, the company HQ had a Bren and Boys ATR and the company's Support Section had three Brens and three Boys ATRs. The company embarked at Leith on 10 May and by the 13th were off Bodø. According to the war diary, the Irish Guards were critical of the Independent Companies, saying they were inadequate at defending positions. The Irish Guards also said that it was difficult to communicate with the Independent Companies and sometimes impossible to know whether they were where they were supposed to be, and that they retired or advanced when it suited them.

British troops from 61st Division being transported from one troop transport to another in a tender off the Norwegian coast, shortly after the first Allied contingents began landing in Norway. The 61st Division HQ staff deployed to Norway to serve as HQ of Maurice Force at Namsos. The Irish Guards were issued with extra heavy clothing for the campaign. They arrived at Harstad on 15 April 1940, disembarking with Arctic coats, sweaters, snow gloves and two kit bags. (© Imperial War Museum, N 56)

French and Polish

The French originally organized the 1re Division Légère de Chasseurs commanded by General Antoine Béthouart with 5e Demi-Brigade de Chasseurs Alpins, 27e Demi-Brigade de Chasseurs Alpins, 13e Demi-Brigade de Légion Étrangère and the Polish Independent Highland Brigade. The 5e Demi-Brigade de Chasseurs Alpins deployed to Namsos. The 27e Demi-Brigade de Chasseurs Alpins had the support of the French 2e Groupe Autonome d'Artillerie Coloniale with three four-gun batteries equipped with the 75mm mle 1897 gun towed by the Laffly S20TL truck. The French 342e Compagnie Autonome de Chars de Combat with 15 H-39 tanks also supported them.

The French 27e Demi-Brigade de Chasseurs Alpins, commanded by Lieutenant-Colonel S. Valentini, was formed at Grenoble at the start of World War I. They were part of 1re Division Légère de Chasseurs on 15 April. They embarked for Norway soon after, and, by 21 April, they were off Scapa Flow. The brigade comprised a command company, a weapons company and three battalions. Each battalion had a command platoon and ski scout platoon, an HQ company, three rifle companies and a support company. There were 3,590 soldiers on establishment, 526 mules, eight wagons, 82 trucks, 76 motorcycles and 34 cycles. French army doctrine throughout the 1930s was based on the primacy of infantry supported by artillery following an elaborate plan. The theory was that such organization would keep casualties low. However, the means needed to control such battles properly

On 23 April 1940, the 4,778-strong Polish Independent Highland Brigade, comprising two demi-brigades each of two battalions, boarded liners bound for Norway to assist with the Norwegian Neutrality Watch. On 5 May, the liners were off Tromsø. The Norwegians had the good sense to persuade the British to deploy them to Narvik. Shown here are soldiers of the Polish Independent Highland Brigade, probably on board the French troopship *Chenonceaux*, en route to Narvik, April–May 1940. They are wearing French Army uniforms and life jackets. (© Imperial War Museum, 109785)

were not sufficient. Fixed communications to equip the Maginot Line and not mobile communications were the priority. A doctrine based on defence suited the emphasis placed upon controlling subordinates. With the army composed of conscripts, officers thought they would be capable of little else. The Chasseurs Alpins had many experienced soldiers and were not as limited by this doctrine as other infantry formations; neither was the French Légion Étrangère. Four Demi-Brigades de Chasseurs Alpins were active prior to the outbreak of war. Ten Demi-Brigades de Chasseurs Alpins had been mobilized by the end of September 1939. Of 27e Demi-Brigade de Chasseurs Alpins, 6e Battalion was already established, stationed at Grenoble, and 12e and 14e Battalion were newly mobilized.

The French 13e Demi-Brigade de Légion Étrangère was formed in February 1940 to fight the Soviets. In the 1930s, many Germans had joined the Légion. Eighty per cent of the NCOs were German and many would bully non-Germans. When the war began, the German legionnaires were sent to remote outposts. The volunteers of the 13e Demi-Brigade de Légion Étrangère, already members of the Légion, were interviewed to assess their motivation for wanting to go on operations. They were experienced soldiers, but had little knowledge of winter campaigning.

During early 1940, the Polish Independent Highland Brigade was formed by France with men who had escaped from Poland when Germany invaded, plus men from the Polish immigrant community that had settled there. They formed two Demi-Brigades each of two battalions, wore French uniforms and were issued with French equipment. The aim was to create an elite formation for operating in harsh environments, as the Allies wanted to free up Norwegian formations from guard duty on the Russian border. Originally they had sailed to Tromsø, because the brigade was raised in France from

Polish exiles to exploit anti-Soviet feeling. However, the Norwegians protested at placing Poles next to Soviet troops. Cork's staff then had the Poles sent to Harstad where they would deploy on operations to fight the Germans. Nevertheless, the motivations of the Poles were honourable and they used French equipment and wore French uniforms.

The Polish Independent Highland Brigade had not had much experience of winter warfare. The soldiers were mostly Polish immigrant workers who had volunteered, commanded by officers who had fought the Germans when Poland was invaded. Two battalions, for the moment, stayed to garrison the Harstad area while the Polish III./Independent Highland Brigade went to Ballangen to support the French and British, and the Polish IV./Independent Highland Brigade went to Salangen. On 16 May, all four battalions were ordered to Ankenes.

GERMAN

Germany first established a *Gebirgs-Brigade* (Mountain Brigade) in 1935. By the start of World War II this was expanded to a division. Austria had much more experience of mountain warfare and following 1918 had kept six mountain regiments and four mountain battalions. These would form 2.Gebirgs-Division and 3.Gebirgs-Division. Each division had two regiments, each with three battalions. Each battalion had a *schwere Kompanie* (4.Kompanie) with two 7.5cm infantry guns, and six 81mm mortars. A *stabs Kompanie* (5.Kompanie) with *Pionier-Zug* (three LMGs) and MG *Zug* (four HMGs) plus three *Gebirgs-Kompanien* (numbered 1 to 3) completed the organization. The *Gebirgs-Kompanie* each had three *Zuge* (with three *Gruppen* each). A signals platoon was with battalion HQ.

Mountain soldiers operated more independently than regular infantry. Battalions each had two 7.5cm infantry guns. Companies had nine LMGs, three 50mm mortars and two HMGs. The allocation of an *sMG-Gruppe* to the *Gebirgsjäger-Kompanie* was done because of the limited lines of sight the soldiers were expected to encounter. Deployment of HMGs to the front of the column did occur, although positioning the guns further back allowed them to support the *Gebirgsjäger* if they had to retreat or were counter-attacked from an unexpected direction. The MGs could also be good at delaying pursuit. Crews were taught to economize on ammunition and identify the most important targets, because of the difficulties of resupply.

A youthful mountain soldier from Gebirgsjäger-Regiment 137 training in January 1940. Gebirgsjäger recruits undertook six months' basic training followed by a year of training centred on learning to operate in hostile environments. A succession of increasingly difficult treks had to be mastered. Scrambling through rock formations was mandatory and some personnel, usually NCOs, were trained with ropes, pitons and links. (Arkiv i Nordland, CC BY-SA 2.0)

Mountain troopers of II./Gebirgsjäger-Regiment 137 by their camp at Krokstranda, 22 May 1940. Self-sufficiency was emphasized among the Gebirgsjäger. *Zeltbahn* shelter-quarters could be placed together to form larger tents and the ability to set them up quickly was essential to survival, especially when operating in freezing temperatures. Building cabins with wood could be done if time allowed. (Arkiv i Nordland, CC BY-SA 2.0)

The three battalions of the *Gebirgs-Artillerie-Regiment* had 16 75mm guns and eight 150mm guns. Artillery was often deployed as individual pieces and was rarely fired by a battery, because of the limited space for deployment and the difficulties of fire control. Artillerymen would be sent out to work out approach routes, gun positions and observation points. Emplacing guns and resupplying ammunition took time. Guns could be camouflaged to cover an unexpected approach, although the abundance of obstacles led to HMGs or mortars being used. The 7.5cm leGebIG 18 split-trail howitzer had a 3,550m range and when dismantled could be carried by ten mules. The 7.5cm GebG 36, a German design, could fire up to 9,250m and was in use by 1939.

Tactics emphasized the control of high ground to stop enemy movement. Combat reconnaissance to identify the best routes and positions in which to place heavy weapons was prioritized. Surprise was essential for a successful attack. Difficult terrain offered better opportunities for surprise, although attackers would be more vulnerable the closer they got to the enemy line, because if the attack was stopped close to the enemy, the Gebirgsjäger, perhaps exhausted and without HMGs occupying proper positions with good lines of sight, could be counter-attacked. This was why the close deployment of the second echelon to the best available cover ready to exploit any success or deal with enemy counter-attacks was important.

As terrain could not always be seen from a single position and there could be issues with radio communication, the influence of platoon commanders could outweigh that of company commanders. Platoon commanders were allowed more latitude, because deploying a company on a single objective was unusual. Those destined to command platoons could be trained as rope leaders, given specialist ski training and were excellent climbers, who were expected to lead soldiers across terrain to make unexpected approaches. Platoon commanders were expected to identify suitable approaches through reconnaissance and work out the best ways to exploit them.

Command and control by battalion and company commanders was emphasized, as they needed to understand the terrain difficulties to best co-ordinate the companies and platoons. Deploying heavy weapons was something they needed to master, especially when preparing defence positions. They also needed to work out the best time to bring them forward when attacking. They would be assigned guns and use signals equipment to co-ordinate fires. Centralized control could be difficult, because of the terrain, and could necessitate assets to be dispersed. Observing targets when the attack got started and maintaining communications could be a problem. Liaison officers were used if the radios were not working. Signals equipment from the battalion accompanied the company commander and the MG and infantry gun platoons. The Torn Fu d2 radio was used with a range of 3.2km (16km if using Morse). Cable could be laid for telephone communication, though when laid on loose snow it frequently broke and needed replacing following a heavy snowfall. High supports, either natural or man-made, could support the line. The use of semaphore signalling and stations to pass on light signals could be employed if the weather was good.

ORDERS OF BATTLE

ALLIED
The below listings for Allied units refer to early May 1940.

NORWEGIAN

6th Brigade (Colonel Loken)
    I./12th Infantry Regiment (Major Bockmann)
    I./16th Infantry Regiment and II./16th Infantry Regiment
    Platoon from 6th Signals Company
    3rd Mountain Artillery Battalion (Lieutenant-Colonel Hornslien)
    Motorized Artillery Battery (Captain Landmark)
7th Brigade (Colonel Faye)
    Alta Battalion (Lieutenant-Colonel Dahl)
    II./15th Infantry Regiment (Major Hyldmo)
    Platoon from 6th Signal Company
    Platoon from 6th Pioneer Company
    3rd Mountain Artillery Battalion, two batteries

FRENCH/POLISH

VI./27e Demi-Brigade de Chasseurs Alpins
XII./27e Demi-Brigade de Chasseurs Alpins
XIV./27e Demi-Brigade de Chasseurs Alpins
2e Groupe Autonome d'Artillerie Coloniale
342e Compagnie Autonome de Chars de Combat
I./13e Demi-Brigade de Légion Étrangère
II./13e Demi-Brigade de Légion Étrangère
Polish Independent Highland Brigade
    1st Demi-Brigade
        1st Battalion
        2nd Battalion
    2nd Demi-Brigade
        3rd Battalion
        4th Battalion

BRITISH

24th (Guards) Brigade
    I./Scots Guards
    I./Irish Guards
    II./South Wales Borderers
    203rd Battery, 51st Royal Artillery Regiment
1st–5th Independent companies

GERMAN

13 MAY 1940

Kampfgruppe Haussels
II./Gebirgsjäger-Regiment 139
2./Gebirgs-Artillerie-Regiment 112 (two 7.5cm guns)
Marine-Bataillon Freytag-Loringhofen (two *Kompanien*)

Marine-Regiment Berger
Holtdorf, Thiele, Zenker, Arnim *Bataillonen*

Kampfgruppe Windisch
I./Gebirgsjäger-Regiment 139 (minus 1./Gebirgsjäger-Regiment 139)
2./Gebirgs-Artillerie-Regiment 112 (two 7.5cm guns)
Kompanie Ploder (3./Gebirgsjäger-Regiment 138)
Kompanie Müller (formed from elements of II./Gebirgsjäger-
    Regiment 139)
Kompanie Schleebrugge (1./Gebirgsjäger-Regiment 139)
III./Gebirgsjäger-Regiment 139
Marine-Bataillon Kothe
Marine-Kompanie Erdmenger (formed from naval personnel)

CHANGES AS AT 27 MAY 1940

Kampfgruppe Haussels had Kompanie Riegler (2./Gebirgsjäger-
    Regiment 137) and Kompanie Schweiger (1./Gebirgsjäger-
    Regiment 137) added.
Kampfgruppe Windisch had established Bataillon Schleebrugge
    (1./Gebirgsjäger-Regiment 139, 3./Gebirgsjäger-Regiment 138
    and 1./Fallschirmjäger-Regiment 1) and had Kompanie Renner
    (2./Gebirgsjäger-Regiment 138) added.

OPPOSING PLANS

ALLIED

Since 1939, the British had been studying the importance of Swedish iron ore to the German war economy. The Industrial Intelligence Centre suggested that if shipments from Narvik could be intercepted the effect on the Germans would be decisive. British long-term strategy was based on the assumption that the Allied economies would outgrow the German economy if they stayed on the defence. While the Joint Planning Sub-Committee (responsible to the Chiefs of Staff Committee) stuck to this belief, the Chiefs of Staff and Churchill wanted to utilize superior British sea power and not get entangled in a costly continental engagement. The Chiefs of Staff suggested that a brigade could deploy on the Narvik–Boden railway and have an effect out of all proportion to its size. They thought a German invasion of Norway was impracticable. However, the Joint Planners disagreed; by December 1939, they thought a German invasion might be on the cards. By emphasizing the threat of Luftwaffe sorties by aircraft deployed to southern Norway, they suggested a larger expedition to stop a German invasion would be necessary and this would need 80,000 men. The Chiefs of Staff were willing to accept the risks inherent in such a large operation. However, they did not tell the War Cabinet of the training and equipment deficiencies of the Territorial Army brigades designated to be the landing force. Also, finding such numbers would be difficult.

On 5 February 1940, the Allied Supreme War Council agreed to land soldiers at Narvik; the force would then occupy the Swedish iron ore mines. British Prime Minister Neville Chamberlain was worried that the operation would have a negative effect on United States opinion, so the operation was postponed. Then Churchill used the interception of the *Altmark* (the German supply ship stopped on 16 February while sailing through Norwegian territorial waters by the destroyer *Cossack*) to ignite debate. He dismissed worries that there would not be enough Allied soldiers to stymie a German landing. The Joint Planners warned that Germany's elite forces would be ready to respond. Again, the Chiefs of Staff did not warn the War Cabinet. The Joint Intelligence Committee warned that 1,200 aircraft could be deployed to counter the Allied landing, though they would not be tasked to scrutinize enemy capabilities. By late March, the War Cabinet agreed that the mine-laying operation – Operation *Wilfrid* – would start on 5 April. This was despite the imminent reopening of the Swedish port of Luleå. The French government were also keen on doing something to establish some sort of credibility and to start a second front as far away from France as possible.

The Chiefs of Staff had also prepared Plan R4 – to land soldiers to capture Norwegian ports when reports of a German landing or intention to land were received. Admiral of the Fleet Sir Dudley Pound would compromise the timely dispatch of the soldiers to Norway when he ordered the disembarkation of the landing force by the early afternoon of 8 April to permit the ships to join the Home Fleet and intercept the German fleet. This he did when Bristol Bleinheim bombers attacked the German ships. Admiral Charles Forbes, commander of the Home Fleet, had raised steam and with the battleships *Rodney* and *Valiant*, the battlecruiser *Repulse* and ten destroyers departed Scapa Flow to intercept what was thought to be a German attempt to sail to the Atlantic shipping routes. The 2nd Cruiser Squadron departed from Rosyth. Forbes had reports that the Germans could be going to land at Narvik. Deputy Chief of the Naval Staff, Vice-Admiral Philips, suggested that these reports were misleading.

Pound, with the mine-laying completed, ordered the eight destroyers to be off Vestfjord at 1007hrs on 8 April, thus leaving the entrance to the fjord open. At 1430hrs, when *Admiral Hipper* was spotted heading north-west to delay the approach to Trondheim, the British thought a break-out attempt was definitely happening. Forbes attempted to intercept by steering north-west, further away from the invasion flotillas approaching Norway. The worsening weather and onset of darkness persuaded him to keep his ships out to sea. While Whitworth, commanding the operation on the battlecruiser *Renown*, was capable of entering the fjord, the destroyers in these weather conditions could not. Forbes sent *Repulse* and some destroyers to assist Whitworth and steamed south at 2000hrs, thinking German ships would be found there. Whitworth, at 1915hrs, belatedly received an order to stop German ships from reaching Narvik. At 2000hrs, Kommodore Bonte with the German destroyers would be where Whitworth had been two and a half hours ago. Whitworth would wait until 0230hrs the next day to order his ships towards the fjord. He soon found out his mistake. At 0337hrs, he encountered the

Narvik and the surrounding area would not have been a base the British fleet could have used to stop the Germans from easily entering the Atlantic, because of German air superiority. Once the Luftwaffe at Trondheim had established decent ground facilities, operating an increasing number of air sorties against shipping based at Harstad was always going to be a threat, and one which Britain did not possess the resources to counter effectively. Here, a crude oil and petrol dump has been hit by a German bomb. (© Imperial War Museum, N 242)

When the German ships departed, the British were already in Norwegian territorial waters. The battlecruiser HMS *Renown* with destroyers *Glowworm*, *Greyhound*, *Hyperion* and *Hero* (shown here), commanded by Vice-Admiral William Whitworth, were off Vestfjord, and the 2nd Destroyer Flotilla, commanded by Captain Warburton-Lee, was protecting 20th Destroyer Flotilla, which was laying mines. (© Imperial War Museum, A 20 A)

German battlecruisers that had decided to use the fog to escape. Whitworth then ordered Warburton-Lee's 2nd Destroyer Squadron to the entrance of the fjord. Bonte had by then passed through.

At 1600hrs on 9 April, Warburton-Lee, off Tranøy lighthouse, realized German soldiers had landed at Narvik, and, joined by the destroyer *Hostile*, decided to attack the German flotilla. He had already received orders from Forbes to land at Narvik at 0952hrs.

Around midday, when the German landing at Narvik was announced by Oslo radio, Pound told Warburton-Lee he was to attack a German ship thought to be there and use his judgement as to whether a landing would be successful. At 1600hrs, the paymaster of *Hardy*, Lieutenant Geoffrey Stanning, was landed with Lieutenant George Heppel at Tranøy lighthouse. They were told that a group of five ships had passed by earlier that day. A Norwegian boy told Stanning that he had also seen a group of ships. Stanning thought that the boy was talking about the same group, but he actually meant another group. The people at the lighthouse warned them to wait for help. However, Whitworth did not send further ships nor did he order Warburton-Lee to wait. Warburton-Lee signalled that he intended to attack at first light on 10 April.

The area of the Ofotfjord experienced long winter months with frequent blizzards piling the snow high. Numerous other fjords struck out from Ofotfjord. The Rombaksfjord was the longest and almost reached the Swedish border. A railway from the town to the Swedish border rose 1,600ft to the Bjørnfjell Pass and then onto the Norddal Bridge to the Swedish border. Defences were rudimentary, comprising two finished blockhouses and unmanned trenches. Colonel Sundlo had been commandant of Narvik since 1933, and he had orders to fire on Germans if they approached the town. Late on 8 April, Major-General Fleischer had ordered I./13th Infantry Regiment to Narvik from the Elvegårdsmoen depot, situated at the end of Herjangsfjord. The 2./13th Infantry Regiment was already garrisoning the town with 6th Engineer Company (minus elements), a 75mm gun, a battery of 40mm Bofors guns and an MG battery. The other companies of the battalion made an exhausting trek through a snowstorm hauling sleighs loaded with heavy equipment. The first men landed at Vassvik Pier at 0130hrs, the last at 0600hrs. Two companies were sent to occupy the blockhouses at Fagernes and Framnesodden, out of sight of the town's buildings and the expected location of any landing. The 1./13th Infantry Regiment was located at the school, and when it approached the railway on the way to town it came face to face with German soldiers who had landed on the pier.

Sundlo was sympathetic to the Nazis, and did not oppose the German landing with determination. He was a supporter of Quisling's National Unity Party and had made plans for a national uprising against the Labour Party.

He held a meeting at 0200hrs to discuss defence plans with the company officers and decided dispositions could wait until first light, as Norwegian patrol ships would warn of any German ships approaching. Commodore Per Askim, commander of the Royal Norwegian Navy at Narvik, comprising two patrol craft, two coastal defence ships and two submarines, had seen a British Admiralty report warning that a German landing at the harbour should be expected. The coastal defence ships were told to ready guns and torpedoes. At 1800hrs on 8 April, Askim was told by the Norwegian Naval Staff that he was to attack any Germans who landed. At 0320hrs the next day, the patrol craft *Kelt* reported nine destroyers at the entrance to Ofotfjord. At 0430hrs, Oslo ordered that if these ships were identified as German, they were to be fired upon. The *Eidsvold* was located just outside the harbour. Sundlo thought it was guarding the entrance to Ofotfjord.

GERMAN

The German landings would, on the whole, be prompted by British policy on Norway.

With the outbreak of war, exports of iron ore from Narvik to Germany fell. Some 762,612 tons were brought from the port from September 1939 to March 1940, which was about one eighth of total exports for 1938. On 29 September 1939, the reluctance of merchant ships to sail was, according to Churchill, a satisfactory state of affairs for which the Royal Navy did not need to prepare any special action. The change to Allied policy that planned a landing at Narvik to assist the Finns during the Winter War was reported to the German leadership by Albert Hagelin, a businessman from Norway and member of the Quisling's National Unity Party. He also suggested that Norway would not resist a German landing. This happened on 5 March; immediately, the Germans accelerated invasion planning.

The surrender of Finland in March 1940 meant that the Allies cancelled the operation. However, the Germans were still aware of Allied intentions to land in Norway. A French officer told Colonel Sundlo of intended landings at Norwegian ports. This was reported to Hagelin, who went to the Germans with this information. On 28 March, a telephone call the French Prime Minister, Reynaud, had about mining Norwegian territorial waters was tapped and reported. He said that the Allies hoped that any mining operations would lead to a German landing, which would then justify a full Allied intervention. This certainly persuaded the Germans of the need to capture Norway. As part of this operation, the seizure of Narvik by a force sailing from Germany was the most ambitious operation the Germans would attempt.

With the knowledge that the Allies had planned a landing, the German leadership still thought they could get to Narvik first. If they were convinced that the Allies would land with the numbers that they thought they would, they must have appreciated the difficulties *Generalleutnant* Dietl would be under. Yet there would be no quick way of helping him. Dietl could not think he was going to be reinforced by sea. With the element of surprise lost, making another landing was not an option. The Luftwaffe could possibly land men at Trondheim. The nearest runway was at Bardufoss, some 70km away. The Germans could only seize it if the Norwegians capitulated completely, but they were not relying on this happening. Gebirgsjäger-Regiment 139 was sent on a mission with the realization that there was no definite chance of success. The regiment did not know for certain they would be stopped by the British, who they knew would be cruising near the Norwegian coast.

Kommodore Bonte, the commander of the destroyer flotilla, knew that if his route to Narvik was blocked he would not have enough fuel to get to Trondheim. When the storm worsened south of the Lofoten Islands, equipment was swept overboard. Nevertheless, he had not seen the British fleet. His destroyers reached the lee of the islands, riding high because of near-empty fuel bunkers. This was when the battlecruisers were sent north-west towards Whitworth. Once at Narvik, Bonte's main concern would be to refuel his ships and sail home.

The oiler *Jan Wellem* had sailed to Narvik from Murmansk; it took eight hours to refuel two destroyers. The other oiler, *Kattegat*, was intercepted and scuttled. Two freighters bringing equipment to Dietl would also be intercepted. Orders stressed to Bonte the importance of not engaging British ships. He radioed to higher authority and to Lütjens commanding the battlecruisers that he would depart after dark on 10 April. The German destroyer captains were not given orders about how to respond if British ships appeared, and they would not know whether to be aggressive or attempt to avoid damage. Bonte was persuaded by Dietl not to sail his ship to Herjangsfjord in order to make communication with him easier.

When Kommodore Bonte died on the torpedoed *Wilhelm Heidkamp*, in the early hours of 10 April, Kapitän zur See Bey took command. Bey was ordered to escape with seaworthy ships. When warned of the impending attack by British battleships and destroyers on 13 April, he was not told whether to fight or scuttle. The sinking of the destroyers by the British fleet would allow Dietl to equip the sailors that had escaped with the weapons and uniforms his men had seized at the depot. Dietl would attempt to expand his area of operations to the north and prepare a defence of the harbour from what he expected would be a British landing.

However, Dietl knew he had little chance of accomplishing his mission. The supply challenges were so acute that he sent most of his destroyers and two battalions to the depot at the end of Herjangsfjord. With only three ships and three companies, he would attempt to capture Narvik. If the Norwegian coastal defence ships opposed him, such a size of force potentially might not be sufficient. With more than a battalion's worth of men defending the harbour area, the Norwegians had a good chance of causing heavy casualties to his force.

Dietl knew he needed to use bluff and guile to dupe the Norwegians into thinking that the government had already capitulated. While Sundlo would be quite receptive to this ruse, Major Omdal with 250 men would march out to defend the railway near the Swedish border. Without the use of this railway, the supply situation for the Germans would be disastrous. Dietl quickly ordered the railway to be secured. The loss of the depot would similarly have limited the immediate sustainability of his force and would not have allowed him to equip the sailors from sunken destroyers. Whether Omdal, if he had stayed there, would have defended or destroyed the depot is not known.

THE BATTLE OF NARVIK

THE GERMAN LANDING AND THE NAVAL BATTLES, 10–13 APRIL 1940

Wilhelm Heidkamp, slowly steaming through murky low cloud and snow showers, at 0415hrs on 9 April, suddenly encountered the Norwegian coastal defence ship *Eidsvold* near the entrance to the harbour. The Germans sent an envoy across to demand her surrender. *Eidsvold*'s captain Willoch radioed Askim to ask what he should do. He was told to refuse the German demand, and when he did the Germans were the first to fire. Dietl had told Bonte not to hesitate. Four torpedoes were launched and two hit *Eidsvold*, causing the ship to sink seconds later, killing 170 crew. The other two German destroyers of the flotilla, *Bernd von Arnim* and *Georg Thiele*, were approaching the quay through the maze of anchored ships and when they presented themselves were fired upon by the two 21cm and six 15cm guns of the coastal defence ship *Norge*. The two salvoes could only bracket the target. *Bernd von Arnim* disembarked soldiers of 2./Gebirgsjäger-Regiment 139 onto the quay from the starboard side while firing its guns from the other side. Torpedoes were launched from both destroyers when the Norwegian ship presented. The seventh hit, sinking the ship minutes later. Ninety-seven crewmen survived.

Soldiers of 7. and 8./Gebirgsjäger-Regiment 139 were also landed from small motorboats and sloops. Dietl expected resistance from the garrison and once he met with the German consul on the pier, he headed to town in a Norwegian taxi with a soldier as his escort. He soon encountered Sundlo by the railway, who was considering what to do after being told he had 30 minutes to decide. Most of the residents appeared on the streets to see what was going on. After the war,

The railway would be an essential supply line for Dietl's men. Sweden agreed to allow a train to go from Germany to the Norwegian border. The train would get to the border on 26 April. Clearing the Bjørnfjell Station of enemy soldiers was completely necessary, as the supplies had to be offloaded at the border. British aircraft had rendered the line to the town unusable by bombing portions of track. (Arkiv i Nordland, CC BY-SA 2.0)

Sundlo would write that the danger to the population was his main concern. He had orders from Fleischer to fight, and when he phoned Harstad to ask what to do, he was told by a staff officer that he had to decide himself. Sundlo, seeing MGs being positioned on higher ground to target his HQ, complied with the request. When Fleischer was notified of this he sacked Sundlo and replaced him with Major Omdal, ordering the battalion to march out of town and defend the railway line.

Major Omdal and 250 men slipped out of town. They could not get any skis or backpacks with supplies. When they got to Bjørnfjell on the Swedish border they pleaded with the Swedes for skis and supplies and they were given some. Omdal and his men would attempt to destroy the 180m-long railway bridge at Norddalsbrua. There would not be enough TNT to completely destroy the bridge, though damage to make it unusable to heavy engines would be achieved. Major Omdal was forced to surrender his force on 16 April when the Germans brought forward Major Schleebrugge's 1./Gebirgsjäger-Regiment 139. The Germans had approached unseen to the east of the Norddalsbrua. The initial attack on Bjørnfjell Station was delayed. When the Germans brought forward a gun on a train to fire on the buildings of Bjørnfjell Station, the Norwegians had no answer. Most surrendered, though some escaped, including Omdal. By early May, the bridge had been strengthened enough to take an engine pushing two carriages to the Swedish border.

Bonte's destroyers started to refuel from the *Jan Wellem*. He positioned three destroyers in Herjangsfjord, two in Ballangenfjord and the others with 25 merchantmen were in Narvik harbour. On the morning of 10 April, *Diether von Roeder* on patrol duty in Ofotfjord did not wait for relief and entered the harbour at 0400hrs. Some 30 minutes later, the British 2nd Destroyer Flotilla, commanded by Captain Warburton-Lee, started to fire torpedoes at the anchored German destroyers. If the path of Warburton-Lee's ships had not been slightly off because of a navigation error, the German guard ship would have encountered them while steaming through Ofotfjord.

Korvettenkapitän Erdmenger, the captain of *Wilhelm Heidkamp*, reported that some shells landed near his ship and then a few seconds later a torpedo hit the stern. Two detonations followed; the second was the most powerful when ammunition exploded. The aft guns were hurled onto the forward part of the ship, smashing on the deck near the forecastle guns. The ship was flooded with smoke and then began to sink. The water got up to the aft funnel and then stopped. No enemy was seen. Exploding shells and the persistent echo the fjords produced made an impression of being fired on from Norwegian batteries located on high ground or being attacked by aircraft. Erdmenger saw a torpedo pass close to the bow and hit the railway pier. Many merchant ships were sinking or starting to burn. He noticed a serious fire on *Diether von Roeder*. A layer of oil hundreds of men were swimming through covered the ice-cold water. When his ship stopped sinking, Erdmenger got the men back on board and gathered on the forecastle. He raised the anchor and brought the ship alongside the Swedish steamer *Oxelösund*. He brought weapons on board the steamer to oppose an expected British landing. Once he realized only five destroyers had attempted the attack, he knew the size of the force was not going to be large enough to capture the town.

At 0430hrs, *Hardy* had fired three torpedoes from 1,500 yards. The first hit a tanker and the second *Wilhelm Heidkamp*, killing Kommodore

Bonte and 80 others. *Anton Schmitt*, waiting to be refuelled by *Jan Wellem*, was hit by two torpedoes from two other destroyers and broke apart. The shock from the second explosion caused the engines of *Hermann Künne*, alongside the oiler, to seize up and the ship drifted towards the wreck of *Anton Schmitt*. *Hans Ludemann*, free from *Jan Wellem*, started a gunnery duel. *Diether von Roeder* was anchored; the destroyer's guns also started a gunnery exchange with the British destroyers, and sustained numerous hits. *Diether von Roeder*'s captain could not get clear, because power to the windlass was interrupted. At 0505hrs he fired eight torpedoes towards the harbour entrance, though none hit. Four British destroyers would report torpedoes running underneath them. Lieutenant Heppel on *Hardy* surmised that this was because the degaussing equipment on the destroyers had stopped the magnetic pistols from working. The torpedoes, set at a depth of between 9ft and 13ft, ran slightly lower through the less salty waters of the fjords. The British destroyers' draft of 12ft 6in and the fact that they were low on fuel also contributed.

The repeated British attack runs gave time for the German destroyers from Herjangsfjord and Ballangenfjord to get underway. At 0553hrs, Bey's destroyers from Herjangsfjord encountered the five British destroyers as they steamed out of harbour. Warburton-Lee was pursued by Bey for 20 miles when the two destroyers from Ballangenfjord could be seen to the front, facing broadside 4,000 yards distant. *Hardy* was soon a burning wreck, Warburton-Lee mortally wounded. Another destroyer lost its steering after numerous hits, and was accidentally rammed by *Hostile* and sank. *Havock* was badly damaged. The Germans broke off the pursuit because they had not completely refuelled. Damage to the two German destroyers, *Georg Thiele* and *Bernd von Arnim*, was not inconsiderable. The ammunition expended by the Germans was not replaced because the supply ships had not appeared. The *Rauenfelds* supply ship was lost when the surviving British destroyers intercepted her on the way out of the fjord. The *Alster* supply ship was lost near Bodø the same day, intercepted by British destroyers.

First and second naval battles of Narvik, 10–13 April 1940

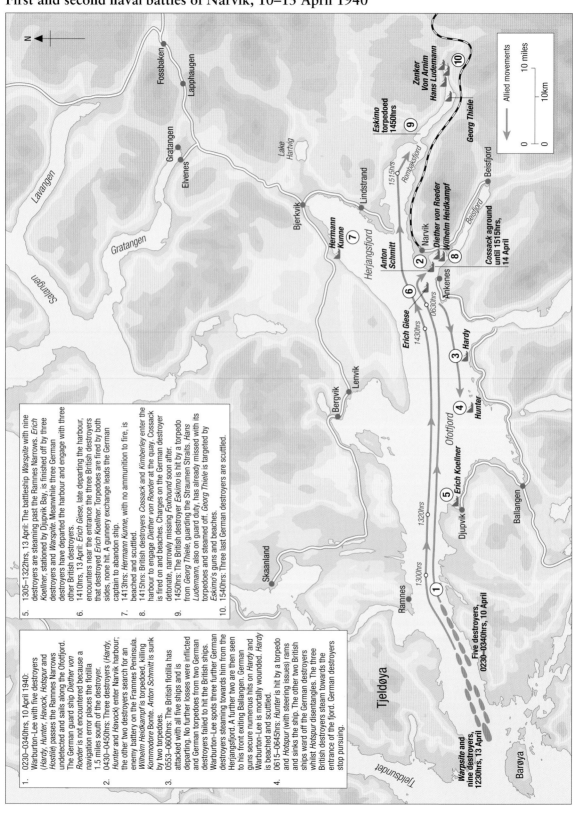

1. 0230–0340hrs, 10 April 1940: Warburton-Lee with five destroyers (Hardy, Hunter, Havock, Hotspur and Hostile) passes the Ramnes Narrows undetected and sails along the Ofotfjord. The German guard ship Diether von Roeder is not encountered because a navigation error places the flotilla 1.5 miles south of the destroyer.

2. 0430–0450hrs: Three destroyers (Hardy, Hunter and Havock) enter Narvik harbour; the other two destroyers search for an enemy battery on the Framnes Peninsula. Wilhelm Heidkampf is torpedoed, killing Kommodore Bonte. Anton Schmitt is sunk by two torpedoes.

3. 0553–0600hrs: The British flotilla has attacked with all five ships and is departing. No further losses were inflicted and German torpedoes from two German destroyers failed to hit the British ships. Warburton-Lee spots three further German destroyers steaming towards him from the Herjangsfjord. A further two are then seen to his front exiting Ballangen. German guns secure numerous hits on Hardy and Warburton-Lee is mortally wounded. Hardy is beached and scuttled.

4. 0615–0645hrs: Hunter is hit by a torpedo and Hotspur (with steering issues) rams and sinks the ship. The other two British ships ward off the German destroyers whilst Hotspur disentangles. The three British destroyers steam towards the entrance of the fjord. German destroyers stop pursuing.

5. 1305–1322hrs, 13 April: The battleship Warspite with nine destroyers are steaming past the Ramnes Narrows. Erich Koellner, stationed by Djupvik Bay, is finished off by three destroyers and Warspite. Meanwhile three German destroyers have departed the harbour and engage with three other British destroyers.

6. 1410hrs, 13 April: Erich Giese, late departing the harbour, encounters near the entrance the three British destroyers that destroyed Erich Koellner. Torpedoes are fired by both sides, none hit. A gunnery exchange leads the German captain to abandon ship.

7. 1413hrs: Hermann Kunne, with no ammunition to fire, is beached and scuttled.

8. 1415hrs: British destroyers Cossack and Kimberley enter the harbour to engage Diether von Roeder at the quay. Cossack is fired on and beaches. Charges on the German destroyer detonate, narrowly missing Foxhound soon after.

9. 1450hrs: The British destroyer Eskimo is hit by a torpedo from Georg Thiele, guarding the Straumen Straits. Hans Ludemann, also on guard duty, has already missed with its torpedoes and steamed off. Georg Thiele is targeted by Eskimo's guns and beaches.

10. 1540hrs: Three last German destroyers are scuttled.

Zenker

Von Arnim

Hans Ludemann ⑩

Eskimo torpedoed 1450hrs ⑨

Georg Thiele

Allied movements

0   10 miles

0   10km

Romdaksfjord

1515hrs

Narvik

Diether von Roeder
Wilhelm Heidkampf

Beisfjord

Anton Schmitt

Hermann Kunne ⑦

② ⑧

Cossack aground until 1515hrs, 14 April

Lindstrand

Beisfjord

Herjangsfjord

Lake Hartvig

Bjerkvik

⑥

Ankenes

0630hrs

Erich Giese

1430hrs

Hardy ③

Lenvik

Bergvik

Hunter ④

Ofotfjord

⑤ **Erich Koellner**

1320hrs

Djupvik

Ballangen

Skaanland

1300hrs

Ramnes

①

Five destroyers, 0230–0340hrs, 10 April

Fossbaken

Lapphaugen

Gratangen

Elvenes

Gratangen

Lavangen

Salangen

Tjeldøya

Warspite and nine destroyers, 1230hrs, 13 April

Tjeldsundet

Barøya

N

Bey soon realized that he was blocked by British reinforcements that had shown up. He got his ships into the best working order and readied himself for the attack German intelligence told him was being prepared. He wanted to disperse his destroyers to the side fjords. On 13 April, he ordered steam raised at 1030hrs, although six ships were slow to get going because of problems with boilers. *Hermann Künne* was escorting *Erich Koellner*, which had no torpedoes and was not seaworthy, to a position from where the British could be ambushed with guns when they appeared. Fairey *Swordfish* floatplanes launched from *Warspite* at 1203hrs spotted *Hermann Künne*. *Erich Koellner* could then be seen taking refuge by Djupvik Bay. By 1322hrs, an unequal duel ended with the sinking of *Erich Koellner* from torpedoes and 15in shells. The crew that survived would be captured.

Hermann Künne, which was sailing to a picket position, was next and sought to lay a smokescreen to let the others hoist anchor and get up steam. Three did this quickly, though two others that were not yet ready stayed put. Five destroyers of the Tribal class were approaching along the northern shore and four of the Forester class along the southern shore. *Warspite* was in between the groups. The three German destroyers sailed diagonally between both sides of the fjord and started to make hit-and-run attacks with torpedoes and guns until 1345hrs. Steadily forced back and nearly without ammunition, a retreat to Rombaksfjord was ordered. Guarded by *Georg Thiele*, late out of harbour, the three ships scuttled after the crews safely made it to shore. *Georg Thiele*, with its last torpedo, inflicted substantial damage on *Eskimo* prior to being run aground on the rocks at Sildvik by 1500hrs. *Hermann Künne*, not receiving the order to retreat to Rombaksfjord, had also run aground on the north shore of Herjangsfjord at 1413hrs, and the crew had no ammunition left. *Erich Giese*, also late of harbour, was fighting five British destroyers and sank at 1430hrs after being hit 22 times. *Diether von Roeder* at the quay and unable to sail was then the target of *Warspite*'s guns as three British destroyers entered the harbour at 1415hrs. *Cossack* was badly damaged and ran aground. The other two veered off when they realized the quay was packed with depth charges. *Diether von Roeder* scuttled when it had exhausted its ammunition. During the battle, 300 German and 83 British sailors died.

A scuttled German destroyer in Rombaksfjord. The crews from the ships scuttled there formed a battalion that was deployed to secure the railway to Sweden. Korvettenkapitän Kothe with the crew of *Hermann Künne* joined Oberst Windisch. The seizure of the Norwegian depot enabled the equipping of 2,600 sailors from scuttled ships with uniforms and weapons. Marine-Bataillon Erdmenger was formed of 500 men from *Anton Schmitt*, *Wilhelm Heidkamp* and *Diether von Roeder*. Sailors mostly defended the least exposed parts of the Narvik perimeter. Those commanded by Korvettenkapitän Loringhoven manned MG positions built from railway sleepers around the harbour. (Arkiv i Nordland, CC BY-SA 2.0)

GERMAN DEPLOYMENTS AND TACTICS

The inhospitable weather and topography offered little in the way of sustenance and threatened to seriously degrade the fighting ability of Dietl's men. A large number of the men had no tarpaulins and were exposed to the constant rainy weather and cold without protection. The rocky terrain did not offer any possibilities of creating shelter. The fog and rain showers with the cold wind made it impossible to stay on high positions. Warm food was not available, because there were no cooking facilities. Hot drinks were difficult to make because of the lack of firewood. The fog permitted the enemy to infiltrate through the defences. Ammunition was strictly rationed, and so was food. Replacements for the wounded or killed were slow to materialize. Dietl would make frequent visits to check on the morale of his men. Pick axes were used on frozen ground or rock to make defence positions, and the soldiers dragged the MGs and mortars up to them through the snow. Men had to be shaken awake to make sure they did not freeze to death.

On 13 April, 12 Ju-52s carrying 2./Gebirgs-Artillerie-Regiment 112 took off from Oslo and, through low cloud on the approaches to Narvik, were fired upon by British ships at 1,000ft, with the loss of three aircraft. With another Ju-52 forced to turn back with mechanical problems, eight aircraft landed on Lake Hartvik, covered in snow. The planes sank into the snow, though the guns and munitions could be recovered, two platoons each of two 7.5cm guns. Radio equipment from the communications aircraft that joined the flight was brought off. No other attempts to land supplies would be attempted on the lake.

On 22 April, British warships targeted the railway, making movement of trains from Sildvik impossible. By then supplies had dried up anyway, and they were not replenished until 26 April.

The Swedish agreed that non-combat equipment could journey through Sweden. However, among the clothes, food and medical supplies, ammunition, weapons and communications equipment were hidden. Also, 290 specialists disguised to look like medical personnel would also be loaded onto the train's 35 railway carriages that travelled through Sweden, arriving on 26 April. On the 27th, 500 men would be sent back to Germany through Sweden on the same train.

The train was essential to Dietl because of the supplies on board. On 22 April, Dietl had 30,000 portions of rations available for his soldiers deployed around the town. Another 30,000 portions were also kept at the Elvegårdsmoen depot. Sildvik had 10,000 for the sailors deployed to guard the railway. These were enough for 14 days. Some 50,000 portions were kept at the depot near the Swedish border out of range of British warships. A ferry had been used to bring supplies over Rombaksfjord to Elvegårdsmoen until 20 April, when it was shot to pieces. On the 26th, the train from Sweden brought 250,000 ration portions. Supplies were unloaded at the border, and they amounted to sufficient sustenance for 4,000 men for three months. A catering camp was set up on the Bjørnfjell. Some 400 men were needed to carry the rations to positions north of Ofotfjord and POWs would be used. The soldiers needed 2,000kg of food a day. Rations were not specially chosen, as ideally they needed to be lightweight, sorted into individual packs and contain plenty of calories.

Dietl expected a landing to capture Narvik and concentrated on strengthening the defences near Narvik and the railway. Guns from the destroyers were brought off, particularly 2cm and 3.7cm weapons. Six 10.5cm guns were also brought ashore, primarily from the British ore steamers. Dietl also made good use of the radio from *Diether von Roeder*, installed on the Fagernesfjell above Narvik. The naval personnel provided technical support, converting the ore railway from electric to steam when the Troeldal power plant was damaged. The Germans seized 48 lorries and a significant amount of petrol from local Norwegians to help with the transportation of supplies.

Gebirgsjäger crossing a fjord on rubber rafts in May 1940. Ferry services on the Rombaksfjord were requisitioned to bring supplies from the depot to Narvik; this went on until 20 April when the ferry was sunk. The ferry across Beisfjord to the Ankenes Peninsula was also seized. Four motor boats found at two small naval support stations would help ferry supplies from float planes that would use the fjord to land on. As the Norwegians had disabled cutters and dinghies, sailors used rowing boats to ferry supplies and personnel across the fjords. (ullstein bild via Getty Images)

Some lorries would be fitted out as ambulances to increase numbers already requisitioned. The ratio of German sick to wounded stood at four to three. Fifty-one men were flown out by flying boat until 25 May and another 87 were brought out by rail to Sweden. The plan was to bring the wounded to Sweden if needed. The two surgeons and two medical officers Dietl had with him had found a modern hospital at Narvik with an outstanding surgeon and plenty of nurses. The building had 80 beds and could accommodate 120 beds if necessary. The German medical officer commended the Norwegian doctors and nurses highly. The Norwegian doctor had experience of treating battlefield wounds. Two heated church rooms were also fitted out to be an emergency hospital with 120 beds for lightly wounded and non-serious illnesses.

The Gebirgsjäger-Regiment battalions each had dressing stations and local sick rooms. The wounded then had to be carried by stretcher a distance of ten miles, which took 18 to 20 hours. German doctors found hardly any infections occurred because of a clean atmosphere both on the battlefield and in the hospital. Some 234 soldiers would be treated at the Narvik hospital until 19 April. When the Rombaksfjord ferry was destroyed the next day, the wounded could not get to the hospital easily. A camp was fitted out as a hospital on Bjørnfjell with 50 beds. Another camp for emergency surgery was built close by with 20 beds. When a hospital at Elvegårdsmoen was captured by the Allies on 13 May, two doctors and 60 sick and wounded were taken prisoner.

Dietl wanted to extend the area occupied to the north of the town to make room for an effective mobile defence. Most of Gebirgsjäger-Regiment 139 had landed at Bjerkvik and on 10 April started to push along the road towards the Oalge Pass. Fleischer needed time to mobilize and bring his battalions forward, as he needed to stop the Germans from reaching Setermoen and Bardufoss. At Harstad he had organized a company of cadets from military schools, including the officers' school. Teachers and instructors were appointed officers. In all, there were 179 men, some as young as 18. On 12 April, they encountered German patrols at Gratangen Tourist Station. They torched the place when a larger German force threatened them with encirclement. On 13 April, Lapphaugen was captured by the Germans when the cadets' commander thought he was going to be encircled again. By the 16th, Elvenes had been captured. The entrance to the Oalge Pass was reached, too.

THE ALLIED LANDINGS AT NARVIK

The first Allied landings at Narvik were planned to secure the railway line to the Swedish border, followed by a march on the Gallivare ore mines expected soon after. On 8 April, the Scots Guards were already embarked. The British Hallamshire Battalion of 146th (Territorial) Brigade was on board another ship with orders to sail to Trondheim. The Scots Guards belonged to Brigadier W. Fraser's British 24th (Guards) Brigade. French and Polish brigades would reinforce the Scots Guards as part of the second echelon of the expedition. Major-General P. Mackesy was the expedition commander. Once the German landings had occurred, the British Hallamshire Battalion was ordered to sail for Narvik with the Scots Guards tasked with seizing an unnamed port close by. Once the ships had got to Scapa Flow, modified orders to seize Narvik using the Norwegian base at Harstad as his first landing place were brought to Mackesy, although he was not to attempt to land against serious opposition until he had sufficient forces. A written note from General Ironside, the Chief of the Imperial General Staff, told him he had an opportunity to exploit the destruction of the German fleet and boldness was required.

Mackesy with two companies of Scots Guards embarked on the cruiser *Southampton* and departed Scapa Flow on 12 April at 1300hrs. He expected to be followed by the rest of the battalion and the British Hallamshire Battalion, followed quickly by four more battalions and two others a week

British soldiers from 61st Division watch the sunset off the Norwegian coast, shortly after the first Allied landings in Norway. Major-General P. Mackesy, the expedition commander, had seen snow at the water's edge as he sailed through the fjords that morning. They looked beautiful, he wrote, though less promising was the prospect of landing and manoeuvring a military force in such conditions. Mackesy expressed reservations to Cork as to the feasibility of a landing at Narvik, wanting to meet personally with Cork before making any decisions. He disembarked at Harstad and established his HQ, while awaiting the transports. (© Imperial War Museum, N 59)

later. Indeed, two brigades had departed the same day on slower ships. Mackesy was to be disappointed when two days later he heard that the British 146th Brigade had been sent to Namsos. Late on 13 April, Whitworth sent a signal suggesting that the expedition be sent straight to Narvik, because the German garrison had been shaken following the sinking of its destroyers and the presence of *Warspite* was keeping them at bay. The next day, he was asked to estimate the strength of the Germans. He answered that they numbered 1,500–2,000 and wrote that Narvik could be stormed without fear of serious opposition on landing. Destroyers with a sufficient number of small guns would be enough support. This was a correct assumption. However, Mackesy's opinion that the garrison was made up of 3,000 soldiers and destroyer crews was wrong. At 1327hrs, he was sent an order from Admiral of the Fleet Lord Cork, who had a copy of Whitworth's signal, to land his 350 Scots Guards with 200 Marines, that Cork could gather from accompanying ships, at Narvik on the morning of 15 April. This message did not get through before the Scots Guards' landing at Sagfjord at the head of Salangen, near the Norwegian HQ on the mainland.

On the morning of 15 April, three large transports escorted by a battleship and nine destroyers arrived off Harstad. Norwegian coastguards had seen *U-49* earlier that morning and reported it to the British. The transports were turned back while a search by the destroyers *Brazen* and *Fearless* was made on the planned route. At 1045hrs *Fearless* had a firm ASDIC contact. Five depth charges were laid and the submarine surfaced. The commander, Kapitänleutnant Curt von Gossler, had lost his nerve; he had experienced another depth charge attack some months ago. He ordered his boat scuttled. *Brazen* approached from a mile distant ready to ram. Once the U-boat crew were seen jumping from the deck, *Brazen*'s commander altered course. While material from the boat was recovered, the British did not realize that the Germans were reading British signals.

By 2100hrs, two transports had been unloaded by Norwegian fishing craft. Then they were moved around to Bygdenfjord to better protect them from submarines. This is when Kapitänleutnant Gunther Prien on *U-47* caught sight of them. At 2242hrs, he fired four torpedoes at the stationary ships from ranges of 750–1,500m. No hits were seen or experienced. At 0136hrs he launched another four at transports 700m distant. One struck a rock, the others did not hit. He turned and ran onto uncharted shallows. The U-boat only got loose when the crew was told to run back and forth to rock the boat. The diesel engine broke from the exertion and had to be mended during the day while the boat rested on the seabed. He had to sail back to base. On the way, *U-47* encountered the battleship *Warspite*, and fired two torpedoes at 900m range. One exploded on the end of its run, alerting the escort who depth-charged the submarine unsuccessfully. The Germans would explain the torpedo failure by pointing to depth-control problems that resulted from leaks to the torpedo's balance chamber and gyro-magnetic problems, because of the iron content of the land, causing the torpedo to run at lower depths and detonate early. Also the Torpedo Department did not conduct the necessary trials on the magnetic firing pistol with four-blade propellers, because of the icy winter conditions.

When no attack on the town could be agreed when Mackesy and Cork met on 16 April, the War Office and the Admiralty told the commanders that

British troops on a transport, accompanied by a destroyer, near the Norwegian coast. German intelligence through signals intercepts was aware that the British intended to build a base at Harstad. Four U-boats were sent to the area: *U-38*, *U-65*, *U-47* and *U-49*. *U-38* and *U-65* at the entrance of the fjord attacked first with torpedoes, but no hits were achieved. The transports were ordered to go through the fjord. I./Irish Guards, the rest of the Scots Guards and Brigade HQ landed safely on 15 April. The II./South Wales Borderers followed the next day. The cargo had not been loaded tactically, so it needed to be sorted out. Each soldier had 35 pieces of clothing, including winter wear. No lorries accompanied the soldiers. (The Print Collector/Alamy)

they should take advantage of *Warspite*'s presence, as the ship would soon be deployed elsewhere. Cork had signalled that no assault could be expected until the snows had melted at about the end of April. However, he did think a landing supported by the ships could work, but he did not communicate this. By contrast, Mackesy did not hesitate to inform the War Office that, in his opinion, an opposed landing would be out of the question, as long as the weather conditions persisted, because his force lacked the landing craft, tanks and sufficient fire support from guns and planes necessary to make it work. The terrain, he wrote, would hamper gunfire support from the ships supporting the soldiers when they cleared the beaches. He told the War Office that he had decided his aim should be the seizure of the peninsulas either side of the town to enable artillery to be directed on German defences. The War Office and the Admiralty pointed out that the French 5e Demi-Brigade de Chasseurs Alpins could not be expected, as they had sailed to Namsos, and the 27e Demi-Brigade de Chasseurs Alpins would not be disembarking until the end of April.

On 20 April, when Cork was made commander in chief of the expedition, the chance of some sort of landing increased. Mackesy wrote to General Ironside, Chief of the Imperial General Staff, that any such landing would lead to the destruction of the Guards Brigade. The Military Co-ordination Committee at Churchill's behest had written to Mackesy saying that he should consider again whether the assault was practicable, because the capture of the town would be an important success. Cork was also told to report whether he was of the opinion that the matter was being dealt with correctly or whether he had other ideas. Cork wrote he had to accept the opinion of his army colleague. Mackesy would only agree to his men landing if a naval bombardment led to the garrison surrendering. The town was to be included in the bombardment, despite the risks to the population. A warning on the radio would encourage them to evacuate.

The Irish Guards brought round to Bogen Inlet on the north side of Ofotfjord, about ten miles from Narvik, stood ready to accept the German surrender. Snowstorms commenced on 20 April and lasted on and off for

Harstad, 12 April–22 May 1940

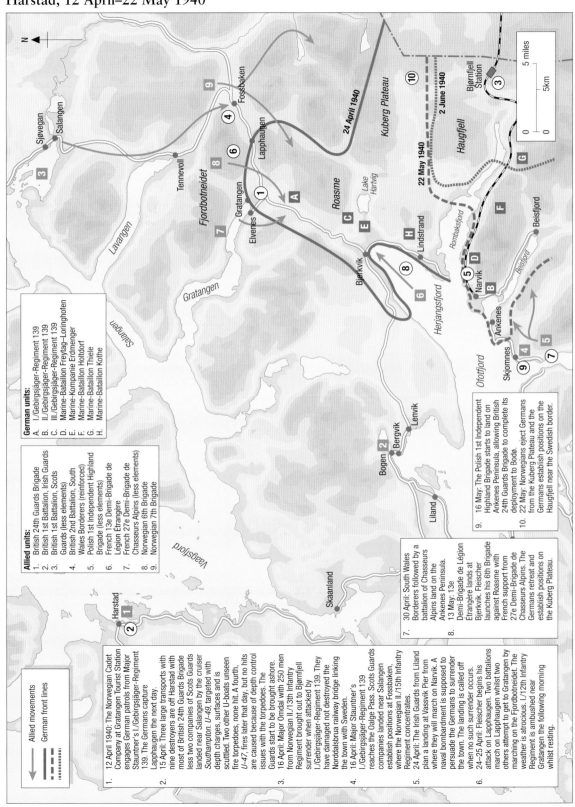

Allied movements ⟶

German front lines ▪▪▪▪

Allied units:
1. British 24th Guards Brigade
2. British 1st Battalion, Irish Guards
3. British 1st Battalion, Scots Guards (less elements)
4. British 2nd Battalion, South Wales Borderers (reinforced)
5. Polish 1st Independent Highland Brigade (less elements)
6. French 13e Demi-Brigade de Légion Étrangère
7. French 27e Demi-Brigade de Chasseurs Alpins (less elements)
8. Norwegian 6th Brigade
9. Norwegian 7th Brigade

German units:
A. I./Gebirgsjäger-Regiment 139
B. II./Gebirgsjäger-Regiment 139
C. III./Gebirgsjäger-Regiment 139
D. Marine-Bataillon Freytag–Loringhofen
E. Marine-Kompanie Erdmenger
F. Marine-Bataillon Holtdorf
G. Marine-Bataillon Thiele
H. Marine-Bataillon Kothe

1. 12 April 1940: The Norwegian Cadet Company at Gratangen Tourist Station engages German patrols from Major Stauntner's I./Gebirgsjäger-Regiment 139. The Germans capture Lapphaugen the next day.

2. 15 April: Three large transports with nine destroyers are off Harstad with most of British 24th Guards Brigade less two companies of Scots Guards landed near Salangen by the cruiser *Southampton*. *U-49*, targeted with depth charges, surfaces and is scuttled. Two other U-boats unseen fire torpedoes, none hit. A fourth, *U-47*, fires later that day, but no hits are caused because of depth control issues with the torpedoes. The Guards start to be brought ashore.

3. 16 April: Major Omdal with 250 men from Norwegian II./13th Infantry Regiment brought out to Bjørnfjell surrender when attacked by I./Gebirgsjäger-Regiment 139. They have damaged but not destroyed the Norddalsbrua railway bridge linking the town with Sweden.

4. 16 April: Major Stauntner's I./Gebirgsjäger-Regiment 139 reaches the Oalge Pass. Scots Guards companies landed near Salangen establish positions at Fossbaken, where the Norwegian II./15th Infantry Regiment concentrates.

5. 24 April: The Irish Guards from Liland plan a landing at Vassvik Pier from where they will march on Narvik. A naval bombardment is supposed to persuade the Germans to surrender the town. The landing is called off when no such surrender occurs.

6. 24–25 April: Fleischer begins his attack on Lapphaugen. Two battalions march on Lapphaugen whilst two others attempt to get to Gratangen by marching on the Fjordbotneidet. The weather is atrocious. I./12th Infantry Regiment is ambushed near Gratangen the following morning whilst resting.

7. 30 April: South Wales Borderers followed by a battalion of Chasseurs Alpins land on the Ankenes Peninsula.

8. 13 May: 13e Demi-Brigade de Légion Étrangère lands at Bjerkvik. Fleischer launches his 6th Brigade against Roasme with French support from 27e Demi-Brigade de Chasseurs Alpins. The Germans retreat and establish positions on the Kuberg Plateau.

9. 16 May: The Polish 1st Independent Highland Brigade starts to land on Ankenes Peninsula, allowing British 24th Guards Brigade to complete its deployment to Bodø.

10. 22 May: Norwegians eject Germans from the Kuberg Plateau and the Germans establish positions on the Haugfjell near the Swedish border.

five days. On 22 April, a Norwegian officer, Lieutenant Kleppe, was back from a clandestine trip to Narvik and reported that there were only 1,000 Germans with few guns near the town. On 23 April, the senior officers of the battalion reconnoitred Narvik harbour on board the destroyer *Bedouin*. The company commanders could see where they were expected to land the next day, following the bombardment. The battalion would land at Vassvik Pier on the north side of the town. The beaches were known to be mined and had MG positions among the rocks. Despite this, 3./Irish Guards and 4./Irish Guards would land and secure a bridgehead. The carrier platoon landing first on the pier would already be on a knoll close by. Then 1./Irish Guards would land and march on the railway line, with 2./Irish Guards landing five hours after the first landing, because of a lack of landing craft, and then march on the town.

It was snowing hard when they went back to Liland. At 0830hrs the next day, when the last man was embarked, a signal was received saying the operation had been called off. Poor visibility that morning had made estimating the effect of the bombardment difficult. The German defenders had withdrawn along the railway. Despite the town being nearly deserted, no landing would be attempted. *Warspite* set sail for Britain. A Norwegian reported that the pier was mined with explosives that would have destroyed the carrier platoon.

Trenches dug 100 yards from the shore with MG positions made a strong defence position. Despite this, Dietl ordered that if a major landing occurred, Oberst Haussels should retreat along the railway and position his men at Sildvik. An engineer flown in on 22 April carried orders that stipulated that the harbour was to be destroyed if a mass enemy landing happened. The demolition began that day and was only not completed because of a shortage of explosives. Whilst the planned Irish landing was problematic, a landing on the east shore of Herjangsfjord to split Windisch off from the town and link with Norwegian forces would probably have met with some success.

On 25 April, Cork signalled the Admiralty that a landing to capture the town was impossible, because snow was still falling. Both Brigadier Fraser and General Béthouart had another plan. The Øyjord Peninsula would be captured first by the Irish Guards and then Framnes Peninsula would be attacked when artillery was established on Øyjord. At the same time, a battalion of French Chasseurs from Bogen would attack on the road to Bjerkvik. This approach would get off to a slow start when the Irish commanding officer had a look at Øyjord and complained that a landing

Polish Independent Highland Brigade troops approach the pier at Harstad, loaded with boxes and equipment. The quays at Harstad were small and to move men between ship and shore, 120 Norwegian fishing craft with engines were put to use as ferries. When German aircraft started to bomb them some days later, the craft would disperse. Most were too small to be targets for bombers, though some were sunk by near misses on the destroyers that were also helping with disembarkation. *Codrington* was the target of bombs; the nearest fell 100ft from the starboard bow. *Electra* was embarking 500 men when a bomber descended to lay a line of bombs nearby. (© Imperial War Museum, HU 109767)

there had no merits. When the South Wales Borderers landed on the Ankenes Peninsula on 30 April, the only casualty was Brigadier Fraser. Lieutenant-Colonel Trappes-Lomax took his place. On 4 May, 25pdrs from British 203rd Battery, 51st Royal Artillery Regiment landed to support them. They started to target the town with high-trajectory shells that would be more dangerous to the garrison and population. A battalion from the French 27e Demi-Brigade de Chasseurs Alpins landed and started to push out with the help of snowshoes on 9 May.

Allied ships docked at Harstad. Note the Sunderland flying boat overhead. Pilots of German bombers soon realized that larger guns on British ships could not be elevated high enough and the smaller guns at higher ranges could not target them. Bombs released from higher altitudes could easily be seen by British observers and the ships could change course to be out of the way by the time they landed. The ships needed to keep the anchor on board and engine running to deal with the German air raids. If a pilot decided to make a low terrain-hugging approach, then the danger increased. When a stick of bombs from a bomber that approached the harbour from low altitude hit a tanker with the destroyer *Echo* alongside, other tankers were stopped from entering the harbour.

On 3 May, with the thaw, Cork wanted to attack Narvik from Rombaksfjord. With only four LCA and four (later six) motor landing craft to lift equipment, British battalion commanders would be cautious. They also complained about the limited number and small size of beaches, the impossibility of achieving surprise, the absence of smoke shells and the threat of aircraft bombing soldiers crowded onto open boats or occupying positions with no entrenchments. Cork, late on 5 May, forwarded the arguments to London for consideration. Before sending a reply, he decided to postpone a landing against Narvik until Mackesy was sent back to Britain. On 7 May, the Irish Guards' commanding officer was shown another beach near the town and refused to land there. No landing took place at Øyjord, so the Irish Guards settled among the Norwegian houses awaiting orders. The Allies' main effort would be made by the Norwegians.

The landing craft would be used to land equipment destined for airfields. On 1 May, a Sunderland flying boat had brought Wing Commander Atchereley to look at suitable airfield sites. The runway at Bardufoss, 75km from Narvik, could be cleared of snow, although the site was 25km from the nearest seaway with only a narrow road joining them, while at the site found at Skaanland, ships could anchor close by. There though, the runway had to be built. At Bardufoss Fleischer sent I./15th Infantry Regiment to help locals clear the snow and build shelters. On 17 May, Cork was told he would get two fighter squadrons.

Glorious and *Furious* with destroyer escorts were off the Lofoten Islands on 18 May with the fighters. Six Walrus flying boats were also on board and would operate at Harstad. The ground crews had landed on 17 May. On the 21st, 18 Gloster Gladiators flew from the carriers to Bardufoss. A flight of Gladiators would fly to Bodø. Bardufoss-based Gladiators would encounter enemy planes on at least 70 occasions. On 26 May at 0830hrs, single-engine fighters flew off the carrier for the first time. Unfortunately, the ground at Skaanland the runway had been built on was too soft. The first aircraft's weight on landing made the ground yield and its wheels got entangled among the wire netting. The landing was stopped and the aircraft were sent to land at Bardufoss.

Gratangen, 24–25 April 1940

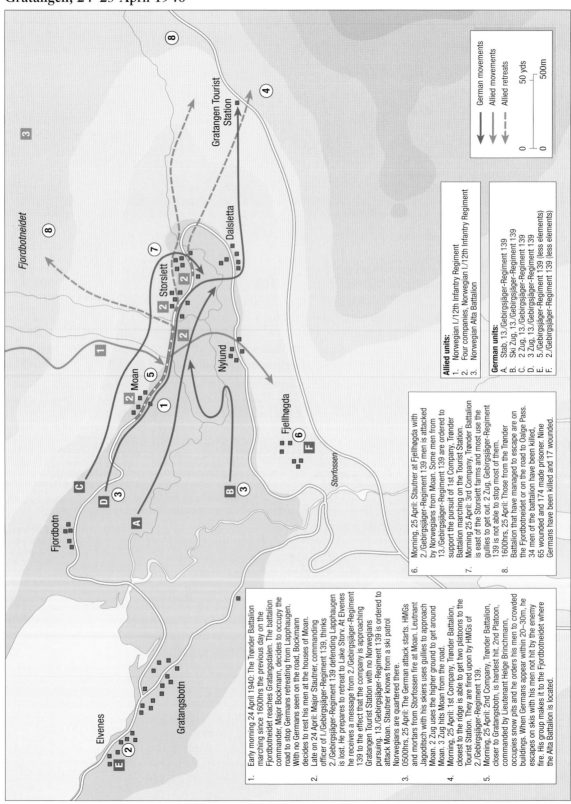

Fjordbotneidet

Gratangen Tourist Station

Dalsletta

Storslett

Moan

Nylund

Fjellhøgda

Storfossen

Fjordboth

Elvenes

Gratangsbotn

German movements
Allied movements
Allied retreats

0   50 yds
0   500m

Allied units:
1. Norwegian I./12th Infantry Regiment
2. Four companies, Norwegian I./12th Infantry Regiment
3. Norwegian Alta Battalion

German units:
A. Stab, 13./Gebirgsjäger-Regiment 139
B. Ski Zug, 13./Gebirgsjäger-Regiment 139
C. 2 Zug, 13./Gebirgsjäger-Regiment 139
D. 3 Zug, 13./Gebirgsjäger-Regiment 139
E. 5./Gebirgsjäger-Regiment 139 (less elements)
F. 2./Gebirgsjäger-Regiment 139 (less elements)

1. Early morning 24 April 1940: The Trønder Battalion marching since 1600hrs the previous day on the Fjordbotneidet reaches Gratangsdalen. The battalion commander, Major Bockmann, decides to occupy the road to stop Germans retreating from Lapphaugen. With no Germans seen on the road, Bockmann decides to rest his men at the houses of Moan.
2. Late on 24 April: Major Stautner, commanding officer of I./Gebirgsjäger-Regiment 139, thinks 2./Gebirgsjäger-Regiment 139 defending Lapphaugen is lost. He prepares to retreat to Lake Storv. At Elvenes he receives a message from 2./Gebirgsjäger-Regiment 139 to the effect that the company is approaching Gratangen Tourist Station with no Norwegians pursuing. 13./Gebirgsjäger-Regiment 139 is ordered to attack Moan. Stautner knows from a ski patrol Norwegians are quartered there.
3. 0500hrs, 25 April: The German attack starts. HMGs and mortars from Storfossen fire at Moan. Leutnant Jagoditsch with his skiers uses gullies to approach Moan. 2 Zug uses the higher ground to get around Moan. 3 Zug hits Moan from the road.
4. Morning, 25 April: 1st Company, Trønder Battalion, closest to the ridge is able to get two platoons to the Tourist Station. They are fired upon by HMGs of 2./Gebirgsjäger-Regiment 139.
5. Morning, 25 April: 2nd Company, Trønder Battalion, closer to Gratangsbotn, is hardest hit. 2nd Platoon, commanded by Lieutenant Helge Brinchmann, occupies snow pits and he orders his men to crowded buildings. When Germans appear within 20–30m, he escapes on skis with his men not hit by the enemy fire. His group makes it to the Fjordbotneidet where the Alta Battalion is located.
6. Morning, 25 April: Stautner at Fjellhøgda with 2./Gebirgsjäger-Regiment 139 men is attacked by Norwegians from Moan. Some men from 13./Gebirgsjäger-Regiment 139 are ordered to support the pursuit of 1st Company. Trønder Battalion marching on the Tourist Station.
7. Morning 25 April: 3rd Company, Trønder Battalion is east of the Storslett farms and most use the gullies to get out. 2 Zug, Gebirgsjäger-Regiment 139 is not able to stop most of them.
8. 1600hrs, 25 April: Those from the Trønder Battalion that have managed to escape are on the Fjordbotneidet or on the road to Oalge Pass. 34 men of the battalion have been killed. 65 wounded and 174 made prisoner. Nine Germans have been killed and 17 wounded.

GRATANGEN, 24–25 APRIL 1940

The Norwegians with Scots Guards at Fossbaken formed a solid defence line. Fossbaken was a road junction and concentration area for Norwegian forces. The rest of the Norwegian II./15th Infantry Regiment arrived quickly, as did guns of Norwegian 7th Battery, 3rd Mountain Artillery Battalion. Fleischer, on 22 April, decided to start his counter-attack the next day at 0000hrs. The Fjordbotn Group, Norwegian I./12th Infantry Regiment supported by the Alta Battalion, would march on the long and high pass called Fjordbotneidet, to Gratangen to stop a German retreat on the road from Lapphaugen. The Kolban Group, with Norwegian II./15th Infantry Regiment, would attack German positions head on at Lapphaugen from Fossbaken, supported by two companies from Norwegian I./16th Infantry Regiment and two MG platoons from the south-east. The guns would support both attacks. However, Mackesy would not permit the Scots to support the Norwegian operation and Fleischer would not allow the inexperienced Norwegian II./16th Infantry Regiment to participate.

Stautner, commanding I./Gebirgsjäger-Regiment 139, organized his positions in 20km-deep echelons, fearing Norwegians on skis would attempt to turn his frontline. 2./Gebirgsjäger-Regiment 139 occupied the Oalge Pass with parts of 5./Gebirgsjäger-Regiment 139 at Elvenes and 13./Gebirgsjäger-Regiment 139 forward of Lake Storv. Snow trenches were dug and contact with the enemy was limited. Oberst Windisch with the regimental staff and III./Gebirgsjäger-Regiment 139, except 13 Kompanie, stayed at Bjerkvik. A platoon carried out patrols along the road to Bogen Bay, observing and deterring Allied landings there. At no time would the Allies try to use this approach to close on German positions once they had landed. The Allies were just as slow to realize the potential of the peaks south of Beisfjord. A German ski patrol was only sent to Ankesfjell on 18 April.

The Norwegian commander, Fleischer, would find it difficult to stop the attack because of the weather, so he decided to continue. Skis got stuck and wet snow clung to them as they drudged upwards to Lapphaugen from Fossbaken. At 0930hrs, the bombardment began. Some 188 rounds were fired. Unfortunately, no effect could be noticed because of the poor weather. Norwegian MGs and mortars were supposed to target German MG positions, but none could be detected. A platoon of the Kolban Group managed to entrench on higher ground enfilading the Germans of 2./Gebirgsjäger-Regiment 139. They would be pulled out and would not see the Germans withdraw later that day. The

The weather worsened with storm-force winds from the south-west as the Norwegians started to march. Sleet with ground slush took the place of snow. Fjordbotn Group, despite being warned by the locals not to attempt it, had marched on the plateau carrying backpacks weighing 30kg and pulling sleighs loaded with supplies. They had completed long patrols on the Finnish border and were equal to the task. Here, the Norwegian I./12th Infantry Regiment are seen training in harsh weather conditions in northern Norway. (Municipal Archives of Trondheim, CC BY-SA 2.0)

companies of I./16th Infantry Regiment would not reach the front, because late orders and the bad weather had delayed them.

2./Gebirgsjäger-Regiment 139 managed to break out and reached the road, although they had to leave the wounded and 81mm mortars. A German skier, who had escaped when his patrol was ambushed, reported the position of the Norwegians to Stautner, though not the position of 2./Gebirgsjäger-Regiment 139. He wrote that the Norwegians occupied the houses close to Elvenes and would probably attack the settlement the following morning. Of more danger was a move on the Gratangseidet. This would go around his positions. Based on the assumption that 2./Gebirgsjäger-Regiment 139 was lost, he decided to position his battalion around 13./Gebirgsjäger-Regiment 139 on the heights near Lake Storv. He went to Elvenes to explain this plan to 5./Gebirgsjäger-Regiment 139 when 2./Gebirgsjäger-Regiment 139 reported on the radio at 2300hrs. Although they did not possess skis or snowshoes, they had escaped the pursuit and thought that they could reach Elvenes early the following morning on the road by the tourist station.

Stautner told them to stay on the radio while he formulated a plan. With the report of Norwegians sleeping by Fjordbotnmark, he decided to bring 13./Gebirgsjäger-Regiment 139 to the front and counter-attack. However, he did not consult the regimental HQ to gain permission. Some 60 skiers would advance from Gratangsbotn to roll up the enemy from the side. HMGs with mortars would cover the road to Lapphaugen from positions close to Storfossen and they would support the attack on Moan. Stautner wanted to order 13./Gebirgsjäger-Regiment 139 through the valley to Moan. The company commander persuaded Stautner that the upper slopes were suitable. This approach would hinder the Trønder Battalion's escape to the Fjordbotneidet.

The attack commenced at 0500hrs. The German columns closer to the buildings at Moan using gullies had not been detected. When a German MG opened up by accident on a Norwegian patrol on the road, the company commander ordered the soldiers to storm the houses. Not many sentries were posted, yet the Norwegians rushed out of the houses to form a firing line. The Germans used grenades at close range to clear the area house by house; not an easy matter as the buildings were dispersed. From the heavy weapons deployed on the heights near the road, the Germans could see the Norwegians leaving the buildings and provided effective covering fire. Meanwhile, 2./Gebirgsjäger-Regiment 139 was supposed to be blocking a Norwegian withdrawal at Fjellhøgda. Stautner went to see if they had reached this position, when some Norwegians began to attack between Moan and Dalstellen. Parts of 13./Gebirgsjäger-Regiment 139 were sent to assist, though this made a weak point near the tourist station and through there many Norwegians escaped. The battle cost Stautner nine dead and 17 wounded. The Norwegians suffered 34 killed, 65 wounded and 174 taken prisoner. German sources state 83 dead, 100 wounded and 208 taken prisoner, many of whom were probably civilians.

Meanwhile, 2nd Platoon of the Norwegian 1./Trønder Battalion had quickly exited the buildings when the firing started, making for alert positions on a ridge 200–300m away through snow that limited the casualties German 50mm mortars could cause. The company commander, Captain Tormod Mitlid, was killed by a mortar bomb that exploded too close to him. Platoon commander Second Lieutenant Kjell Dyblie took his place. Two platoons got to the crest by the tourist station and took up positions facing the road on the ridge. They fired at Germans approaching on the road when the weather cleared a little, though they started to be hit by fire from the other side, suggesting that they would soon be surrounded. They ran towards the forest and used stone boulders on a rocky ledge for cover.

Unfortunately, the Norwegian Alta Battalion located on the Fjordbotneidet did not help. Poor communication and a lack of situational awareness was the cause. The Alta Battalion might have fired upon the Norwegian Trønder Battalion by accident. They had heard that Germans had seized uniforms from the depot. The Germans were using hostages when they attacked the Trønder Battalion; perhaps the Alta Battalion thought they were disguised Germans. The use of hostages did not offer them much success, as the German soldiers who used them as human shields were still fired upon by snipers and hit.

Captain Mjoen's 3rd Company was not as badly damaged because he had ordered them to the valley floor just before the firing started. Some were caught when exposed and were pinned down momentarily. The commander of 1st Platoon, Lieutenant Helge Wiig, decided he had had enough and deserted. He would later join the Norwegians fighting with the Germans.

While the Norwegians would capture Gratangen and Lapphaugen on 27 April despite this defeat, the thaw limited further attacks. Fleischer then organized the Norwegian 6th and 7th brigades. Oberst Loken commanded the Norwegian 6th Brigade with both battalions of the Norwegian 16th Infantry Regiment and the damaged Trønder Battalion. The Norwegian 7th Brigade commanded by Oberst Faye had the Norwegian Alta Battalion and the Norwegian II./15th Infantry Regiment. On 30 April, the French 6e Bataillon de Chasseurs Alpins was brought to Gratangen. The Bataillon's HQ was established at the houses on Fjellhøgda next to the Norwegian 7th Brigade. The Germans realized that the Norwegians could rapidly manoeuvre on skis and did not need roads, so they intended to occupy the high ground to stop any Norwegian attack. On such locations would the next battles be fought.

BRINCHMANN'S NORWEGIANS WITHDRAW FROM MOAN, 25 APRIL 1940 (PP. 44–45)

At Moan, the Norwegian 2nd Platoon, 2nd Company, Trønder Battalion commanded by Lieutenant Helge Brinchmann (**1**), had dug snow pits, and he had posted guards. At 0430hrs, they reported movement at the boarding school 400–500m away. Brinchmann raised the alarm. He sent a warning to the company commander and 1st Platoon stationed 100m from his position. No enemy could be seen because of the darkness. Then at 0500hrs mortar bombs started to land on the camp. Machine-gun fire from two directions made his platoon's snow positions untenable and he sent them to some buildings. They were soon crowded out and Brinchmann told a section to sprint to the rest of the company positions. Some were hit and wounded. Others had started to leave the buildings without waiting to be ordered to do so.

The Germans were slowly getting closer; when they appeared within 20–30m, Brinchmann and some others strapped on skis and with no kit bags on dashed out. The scene depicts Brinchmann and his men as they start to pull back. A machine gunner armed with a Madsen (**2**) provides covering fire, as the loader (**3**) prepares a fresh magazine for him. A mortar round has landed near their positions (**4**). The other Norwegian infantry are armed with the Krag–Jørgensen 1894 6.5mm rifle (**5**). All the Norwegians wear white camouflage smocks.

Brinchmann and most of his group got out safely and made it to Fjordbotneidet. 2nd Company lost ten killed, 17 wounded and 67 missing.

BEISFJORD

Instead of assaulting Narvik following the bombardment, the Allies opted to approach from the south. From Bogen, two battalions of British and French soldiers started to move by boat to the Ankenes coastal road and then Beisfjord. Attacks on 6./Gebirgsjäger-Regiment 139 – deployed to the peninsula on 1 May – started to intensify. On 6 May, point 295 was captured. British 25pdr guns deployed to support the battalions could target the ferry to Ankenes. On 10 May, Haussels sent 7./Gebirgsjäger-Regiment 139 to Beisfjord by lorry; they then climbed to point 606 and other peaks. Two 81mm mortars were set up on the other side of the crest of point 606. The positions of 7./Gebirgsjäger-Regiment 139 would not be attacked until late May when the attack on Narvik started. The British and French could not advance directly to the ferry at Beisfjord. Instead they moved on Ankenesfjell. Polish battalions then replaced the British and French by mid-May and this lull permitted the Germans to establish firmer positions on Ankenesfjell.

At 0130hrs on 16 May, eight small boats loaded with the first of the Polish soldiers could be seen near the Framnes Peninsula; the destination was Ankenes. From a 2cm gun at Framnes and HMGs near Ankenes, the boats took heavy fire and turned off, landing safely further away. The two German companies on this side of Beisfjord were so weak that they could only occupy positions with four to five men 500m from each other. The Poles, once established on high ground, could target them at leisure. The numerous gullies permitted the Poles to approach undetected. The Germans built small shelters of stones. With few places to retreat to, 6./Gebirgsjäger-Regiment 139 was especially vulnerable. Ammunition resupply mostly by naval personnel was done with great difficulty, as the route was under constant observation. The soldiers on the frontline were told to limit ammunition use. Following repeated attacks, 6./Gebirgsjäger-Regiment 139 was pulled out during the early hours of 19 May. Then 8./Gebirgsjäger-Regiment 139 occupied the positions and soon had to fight a Polish battalion-sized attack later that day.

Hauptmann Salzer wrote about the attacks on his men on 24 May. The nine men of Group K experienced mortar and HMG fire when the fog lifted. Then, suddenly, LMGs from a Polish company that had worked its way forward opened up. Using boulders for cover, the Poles crept closer and threw some hand grenades towards the German entrenchments. A runner was sent 600m in order to summon help. Then the first soldier was fatally shot and rolled down the hillside. Another was shot in the neck and wounded. The section's LMGs fired well-aimed bursts. The first gunner was shot in the chest and sank back. The second LMG still maintained a steady fire. The Poles had managed to occupy dead ground and the section commander decided to leap forward and throw a grenade. He was shot by a sniper and rolled down

The Narvik harbour basin on 5 May 1940. If the Allies could establish a position on the other side of the Beisfjord, they could fire upon the harbour. By late April Major Haussels organized a platoon of gunners with Norwegian heavy MGs supported by skiers to point 606 to deter the approach to the end of Beisfjord. On 1 May, he sent 6./Gebirgsjäger-Regiment 139 commanded by Oberleutnant Obersteiner to Fagernes, from where they were rowed to a position near Ankenes. The village was captured, though British destroyers halted the further advance on Emmenes. When the Allies took point 295, they had excellent lines of sight to Narvik. The Germans had to hold onto the steep mountainsides surrounding the Beisfjord. By mid-May, heavy weapons could target the road running along the shore of the Beisfjord and German floatplanes could no longer use it. (ullstein bild via Getty Images)

the slope. The second machine gunner was then wounded. The other LMG started to fire again when the wounded gunner crawled back to his weapon. The runner returned and helped him on the gun, having survived enemy fire on his return trip. Soon an officer with the neighbouring section rushed in, attacking the enemy from the side and forcing him back to his lines. Reinforcements were drip fed to Salzer by Haussels, including men from his signals and pioneer platoons. Naval personnel would also be brought over and integrated with the mountain infantryman. To bring it up to strength, 8./Gebirgsjäger-Regiment 139 was reinforced with about 160 men, equipped with five HMGs, three 81mm mortars and one 3.7cm AT gun. Haussels was able to do this because the threat to Narvik itself had dissipated.

Opposite 7./Gebirgsjäger-Regiment 139, the Poles did not launch attacks until 27 May, by when they had two battalions. Polish prisoners informed the Germans that Ankenes was to be attacked imminently, at the same time as the landing from Rombaksfjord to seize Narvik. Once the Allied intentions were confirmed by Luftwaffe intelligence reports, 1. and 2./Gebirgsjäger-Regiment 137, who had landed by parachute (shown here) after a crash course, were allocated to assist the Narvik garrison. Haussels assigned 2.Kompanie to Ankenes, despite Dietl's disapproval. Dietl would obtain 1,700 soldiers landed mostly by parachute or seaplane with some also disguised on board trains from Sweden. (Sueddeutsche Zeitung Photo/Alamy)

GRESSDALEN AND ROASME, 1–13 MAY 1940

On the morning of 27 April, the Allies targeted the supply line from Bjerkvik to Elvenes with bombardment. A cruiser destroyed two barracks at the army depot. The bombardment was intended to disrupt supply lines prior to attacking the right flank of Kampfgruppe Windisch. Windisch had most of I./Gebirgsjäger-Regiment 139 covering the Bjerkvik–Fossbakken road. Meanwhile, III./Gebirgsjäger-Regiment 139 was mostly held north of Lake Hartvik as reserve. Gressdalen on the right was not a main position, occupied only by a platoon. If the Allies could break through there, they could outflank Windisch's main body on the road and isolate them from the rest of Dietl's command. Windisch considered Herjangsfjord his main priority, as he expected an enemy landing. When Norwegians on skis were sighted, Dietl realized that the Norwegians wanted to capture Gressdalen. On 30 April, he sent 1./Gebirgsjäger-Regiment 139 to help.

On 1 May, the Norwegian 6th Brigade launched the two battalions of 16th Infantry Regiment against the Germans on Gressdalen from Lapphaugen and then marched on the depot. Gressdalen is a 7km-long, treeless valley with a lake at the middle and steep, sloped mountains on either side. At the southern end it falls steeply to Vassdalen. The Britatind (1,009m) and Stortind (1,150m) peaks were on the western side. Neither 6th nor 7th Brigade thought they needed to find out if German soldiers had occupied them. The Norwegian II./16th Infantry Regiment was not issued with snow camouflage suits, although they did use skis. They were soon targeted by German MG fire from Britatind as they skied along the western bank of the lake. The Norwegian I./16th Infantry Regiment skied along the eastern bank,

Roasme and Bjerkvik, 1–13 May 1940

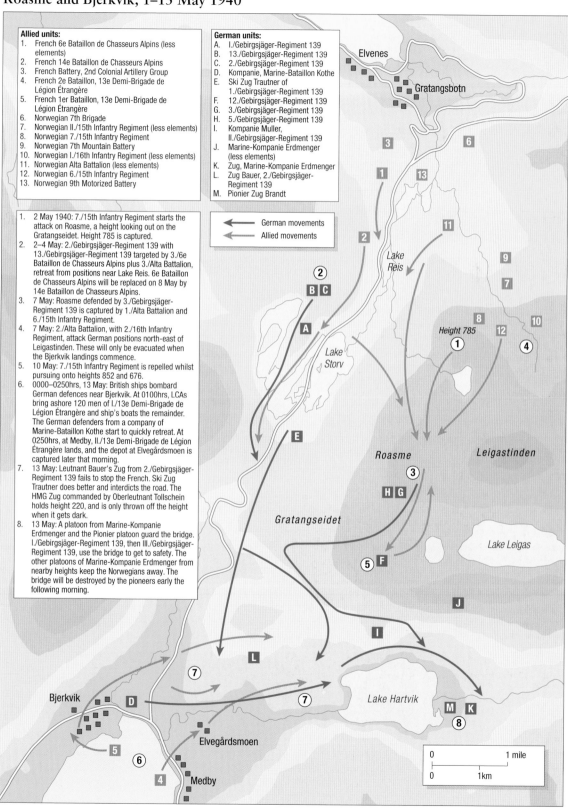

Allied units:
1. French 6e Bataillon de Chasseurs Alpins (less elements)
2. French 14e Bataillon de Chasseurs Alpins
3. French Battery, 2nd Colonial Artillery Group
4. French 2e Bataillon, 13e Demi-Brigade de Légion Étrangère
5. French 1er Bataillon, 13e Demi-Brigade de Légion Étrangère
6. Norwegian 7th Brigade
7. Norwegian II./15th Infantry Regiment (less elements)
8. Norwegian 7./15th Infantry Regiment
9. Norwegian 7th Mountain Battery
10. Norwegian I./16th Infantry Regiment (less elements)
11. Norwegian Alta Battalion (less elements)
12. Norwegian 6./15th Infantry Regiment
13. Norwegian 9th Motorized Battery

German units:
A. I./Gebirgsjäger-Regiment 139
B. 13./Gebirgsjäger-Regiment 139
C. 2./Gebirgsjäger-Regiment 139
D. Kompanie, Marine-Bataillon Kothe
E. Ski Zug Trautner of 1./Gebirgsjäger-Regiment 139
F. 12./Gebirgsjäger-Regiment 139
G. 3./Gebirgsjäger-Regiment 139
H. 5./Gebirgsjäger-Regiment 139
I. Kompanie Muller, II./Gebirgsjäger-Regiment 139
J. Marine-Kompanie Erdmenger (less elements)
K. Zug, Marine-Kompanie Erdmenger
L. Zug Bauer, 2./Gebirgsjäger-Regiment 139
M. Pionier Zug Brandt

German movements
Allied movements

1. 2 May 1940: 7./15th Infantry Regiment starts the attack on Roasme, a height looking out on the Gratangseidet. Height 785 is captured.
2. 2–4 May: 2./Gebirgsjäger-Regiment 139 with 13./Gebirgsjäger-Regiment 139 targeted by 3./6e Bataillon de Chasseurs Alpins plus 3./Alta Battalion, retreat from positions near Lake Reis. 6e Bataillon de Chasseurs Alpins will be replaced on 8 May by 14e Bataillon de Chasseurs Alpins.
3. 7 May: Roasme defended by 3./Gebirgsjäger-Regiment 139 is captured by 1./Alta Battalion and 6./15th Infantry Regiment.
4. 7 May: 2./Alta Battalion, with 2./16th Infantry Regiment, attack German positions north-east of Leigastinden. These will only be evacuated when the Bjerkvik landings commence.
5. 10 May: 7./15th Infantry Regiment is repelled whilst pursuing onto heights 852 and 676.
6. 0000–0250hrs, 13 May: British ships bombard German defences near Bjerkvik. At 0100hrs, LCAs bring ashore 120 men of I./13e Demi-Brigade de Légion Étrangère and ship's boats the remainder. The German defenders from a company of Marine-Bataillon Kothe start to quickly retreat. At 0250hrs, at Medby, II./13e Demi-Brigade de Légion Étrangère lands, and the depot at Elvegårdsmoen is captured later that morning.
7. 13 May: Leutnant Bauer's Zug from 2./Gebirgsjäger-Regiment 139 fails to stop the French. Ski Zug Trautner does better and interdicts the road. The HMG Zug commanded by Oberleutnant Tollschein holds height 220, and is only thrown off the height when it gets dark.
8. 13 May: A platoon from Marine-Kompanie Erdmenger and the Pionier platoon guard the bridge. I./Gebirgsjäger-Regiment 139, then III./Gebirgsjäger-Regiment 139, use the bridge to get to safety. The other platoons of Marine-Kompanie Erdmenger from nearby heights keep the Norwegians away. The bridge will be destroyed by the pioneers early the following morning.

further away from the peak. Guns of the Norwegian 8th Mountain Battery targeted the German MGs on the peak. When 1./Gebirgsjäger-Regiment 139 arrived, German Ski Zug Bussmer was told to occupy the Britatind peak above Gressdalen to attack the Norwegians from the side, while the rest of the company occupied positions to the south of the lake. While Bussmer occupied Britatind, the Norwegian Alta Battalion would throw him off on 7 May by attacking from the other side of the hill.

On 2 May, German positions on the saddle at the southern end of the lake could see the Norwegians setting up camp to the north of the lake. At 0400hrs on 4 May, the Norwegian I./16th Infantry Regiment skied along the eastern side of the lake. The attack on 1./Gebirgsjäger-Regiment 139 was thrown back as was another the next day. Instead the Norwegians shifted onto the rocky slopes of Bukkefjell, located to the east of the lake. Dietl's worries about a wide sweep around to the Swedish border were about to be realized. In addition to 1./Gebirgsjäger-Regiment 139, on 1 May Dietl had ordered Kompanie Müller from II./Gebirgsjäger-Regiment 139 to Lake Hartvik, as well as Marine-Kompanie Erdmenger. The companies marched during the early hours when the ice was frozen. On 5 May, the Norwegian I./16th Infantry Regiment was pulled out of the line and the Norwegian II./16th Infantry Regiment took its place. By 7 May, German positions were forced off the southern shore of the lake.

Meanwhile I./Gebirgsjäger-Regiment 139 had witnessed the landing of French Alpine elements on the southern shore of Gratangsbotn, completed on 1 May. The Norwegian 7th Brigade would be supported by the 6e Bataillon de Chasseurs Alpins while attacking Roasme, a height on the eastern side of the Gratangseidet. The Norwegian II./15th Infantry Regiment led the attack on 2 May. On the left the Norwegian Alta Battalion would march on Leigasskardet at the foot of Leigastinden. On 2 May, Norwegians of 7./15th Infantry Regiment took the northern point, peak 785, of the Roasme Plateau. The Norwegian skiers had approached the tree line through fog. When they

Shown here are French and Norwegian troops preparing to evacuate. The French 27e Demi-Brigade de Chasseurs Alpins had landed at Sjøvegan. However, with only 70 skiers per battalion and lacking mules and snowshoes, the ability of the French to manoeuvre was limited. Some, especially the French 6e Bataillon, also lacked experience of camping in winter weather. The French mostly did not possess skis and needed the Norwegian companies' support. The French 6e Bataillon de Chasseurs Alpins would soon be pulled out, to be replaced by the 14e Bataillon de Chasseurs Alpins. (© Imperial War Museum, N 160)

emerged at the foot of a lofty knoll, German MGs opened fire. The skiers took cover while the Norwegian heavy weapons company responded to the defenders' fire. Then 2nd Platoon stormed the height. German positions pulled back to the Roasme Peak. Elsewhere on 4 May, 2./Gebirgsjäger-Regiment 139 and 13./Gebirgsjäger-Regiment 139 were attacked south of Lake Reis. Ski Zug Trautner used hit-and-run tactics to make it appear that larger forces intended to threaten the Norwegians from the side and the German front held. Not as successful were elements of 12./Gebirgsjäger-Regiment 139 (20 men) held as the reserve and brought forward to attack height 785; they were captured by Norwegian ski patrols.

Dietl needed to shorten the frontline and create local reserves. I./Gebirgsjäger-Regiment 139 on 7 May occupied positions to the south of Lake Storv and Roasme. 13./Gebirgsjäger-Regiment 139 was positioned as the reserve as 1./Gebirgsjäger-Regiment 139 was sent to Kuberg to deter the wider sweeping manoeuvre Dietl still worried about. Marine-Bataillon Kothe also relieved 3./Gebirgsjäger-Regiment 139 on coastal defence duties on Herjangsfjord with a company. A 3./Gebirgsjäger-Regiment 139 platoon occupied Roasme Peak (856m), between I. and III./Gebirgsjäger-Regiment 139. On 7 May, Roasme was attacked and, with fog concealing the approach, quickly captured. Through 2m of snow the Germans had to form a line further back on the morning of 8 May. 12./Gebirgsjäger-Regiment 139 was called upon to intercept the Norwegian 7./15th Infantry Regiment pursuing the Germans near heights 852 and 676 on 10 May.

Another battle was being played out on the Leigasskaret 800m-high pass leading to Lake Leigas. The Norwegian 2./Alta Battalion and 2./16th Infantry Regiment had the task of capturing the pass starting on 3 May. On 7 May, Norwegian snipers from the top of Britatind located the German positions. The peaks were the most inhospitable of locations, with only a small amount of snow, as most had been swept away by the strong winds. Keeping warm was near impossible, as firewood was not available. With German artillery harassing them from the front and German ships in Herjangsfjord behind them, the soldiers had to contend with the pernicious danger of bombardment at all times of the day. On 13 May, German positions were vacated as news of the landing at Bjerkvik was received.

By 12 May, Windisch, with 900 men, was facing about 5,000 Norwegian and 1,000 French soldiers. I./Gebirgsjäger-Regiment 139 with 5. and 3./Gebirgsjäger-Regiment 139 south of Roasme and 2./Gebirgsjäger-Regiment 139 with Ski Zug Trautner near the road had 13./Gebirgsjäger-Regiment 139 in reserve. III./Gebirgsjäger-Regiment 139 had two of its companies with Marine-Kompanie Erdmenger at point 852 and point 768. Kompanie Müller was the reserve north of Lake Hartvik where the supplies were being kept. With Roasme captured, the French 14e Bataillon de Chasseurs Alpins had a good chance to march along the road north of Lake Storv. A landing at Bjerkvik by the French Légion Étrangère was to be more effective.

THE BJERKVIK LANDING, 13 MAY 1940

On 12 May, a fresh snowfall had left 25cm of snow on the shoreline of Herjangsfjord. Ofotfjord began to fill with ships. At midnight, the bombardment by the fleet started, lasting until 0200hrs. Houses were

The II./Polish Independent Highland Brigade would support the French Légion Étrangère landing at Bjerkvik by marching on the latter from Bogen, as shown here on 13 May 1940. (© Imperial War Museum, HU 128127)

targeted, despite not being occupied by German defenders. With the coastline blanketed with billowing smoke and buildings by the shoreline burning, the landing craft approached with 120 French Légion Étrangère soldiers; others were being brought ashore by boat. The majority of the defenders, elements of a naval company from German Marine-Bataillon Kothe, fell back; some held position to momentarily fire at disembarking French infantry. The German divisional war diary blamed the company commander for withdrawing his sailors without noticeable enemy pressure. The company departed the position, leaving its heavier weapons. When the French were established on the beaches, there was little they could do.

Two battalions of the French Légion Étrangère had landed either side of Bjerkvik and the depot was quickly captured; other forces moved by road to Elvenes. Windisch had to retreat eastwards while being attacked by the French and the Norwegians from the north. He also had to bring along as much of the supplies as possible. At 0400hrs on 13 May, Leutnant Bauer, with 30 men from 2./Gebirgsjäger-Regiment 139, was ordered to halt the pursuit before the French reached Lake Hartvik. German Ski Zug Trautner with elements of 13./Gebirgsjäger-Regiment 139, were ordered to join him. Unable to reach Bauer before the platoon was overrun, they did manage to interdict the roads to the lake and Elvenes. Twenty men with three HMGs, commanded by Oberleutnant Tollschein, then stopped the pursuit in its tracks from point 220. A minefield blew the tracks off the tanks approaching on the snow-covered road. At night the French attempted to seize point 220; bounding

The Allied shelling of Bjerkvik started at 0000hrs on 13 April 1940. The small wooden houses of the settlement were quickly set on fire, especially when ammunition stores were hit. (ullstein bild via Getty Images)

figures in grey anoraks were targeted by accurate shooting as they approached the peak. Grenades started to fly into the German positions and the five *Gebirgsjäger* that survived realized that it was time to depart. The high rocky cliff that the French had not climbed up was the only way out. Instinctively they jumped, flying through the air for 60m, landing in a snowdrift.

On 13 May, a platoon of German Marine-Kompanie Erdmenger was detailed to guard the bridge across the Vasdalelven. The regimental pioneer platoon was also sent

there. The Germans of Stautner's I./Gebirgsjäger-Regiment 139 then III./Gebirgsjäger-Regiment 139 had to disengage from the Norwegians. All had to cross the bridge on 13 May. Despite being visible from Herjangsfjord, the men were not fired upon. Both French and Norwegians might have mistaken them for friendly forces. Twenty-five men with two HMGs and four LMGs from Marine-Kompanie Erdmenger kept the Norwegians at bay from positions overlooking Gressdalen to allow III./Gebirgsjäger-Regiment 139 to disengage. The depot on Lake Hartvik could not be brought out, so it was destroyed. As no vehicles or sleds were available, Stautner's I./Gebirgsjäger-Regiment 139 lost five 81mm mortars, two infantry guns and two mountain guns. By 0400hrs on 14 May, the pioneers had blown up the bridge. Windisch's men were too exhausted to build new positions or climb the heights. The French pursuit was lethargic and French attempts on points 482 and 548 were repulsed by elements of 13./Gebirgsjäger-Regiment 139 and Kompanie Müller. On 15 May, Norwegians captured point 717 from 12./Gebirgsjäger-Regiment 139.

STAUTNER ON THE LITLEBALAK POSITION, 22 MAY 1940

When Colonel Berg took command of the Norwegian 6th Brigade, he wanted them to attack eastwards toward the Swedish border. Dietl had to form a new line along the mountain ridges to stop him. The area of operations would be known as the Kuberg Plateau with peaks of 1,000m and more. The Germans were helped by the double-wired cable found at the Norwegian depot. With this they established good communications.

The Norwegians of II./16th Infantry Regiment started to attack German positions on 14 May from Bukkedalen. On the 17th, 6./16th Infantry Regiment with 5./16th Infantry Regiment marched on Kopperfjell. A mountain ridge was cleared on 18 May. Heavy fog then descended, causing the operation to be temporarily postponed until late on the 20th.

Allied LCAs make their way to shore at Bjerkvik. At 0100hrs, when the landing of the French I./13e Demi-Brigade de Légion Étrangère commenced, the bombardment was switched from the shoreline to other targets. The pier was destroyed and this made boats land to the left of Bjerkvik. A tank on the beach fired at some German positions. The second tank started to approach the Gratangen road. A break occurred and then the bombardment began again to cover the landing of the French II./13e Demi-Brigade de Légion Étrangère at 0250hrs near Meby. The aircraft flying from *Ark Royal* appeared once the low cloud had dissipated. Two LCMs on *Resolution* were slowly being hoisted from the deck. They arrived late with the second landing and the tanks helped storm the depot buildings later that day. The population had departed when a warning of a landing was issued; many went back when the German garrison started to depart. Fourteen people were killed and many others wounded; some were killed when the French legionnaires stormed the buildings. (© Imperial War Museum, HU 93723)

The I./Gebirgsjäger-Regiment 139 was situated around Lake Fisklo; looking over the position was the 572m Litlebalak. Stautner was of the opinion that III./Gebirgsjäger-Regiment 139 to his north had placed too few men from 15./Gebirgsjäger-Regiment 139 on this height. He made the decision to place 2 Zug from his reserve company (Kompanie Müller) with an HMG group to the north-east of the height. When on 17 May regimental HQ ordered Kompanie Müller to the left of Stautner's position, because the Chasseurs Alpins were expected to attack there, 2 Zug north-east of Litlebalak were to go with them. Stautner delayed the deployment until 20 May, on the same day that Litlebalak was attacked. They were sent back to Litlebalak to help. Two Norwegian companies from Alta Battalion from Lake Hartvik had broken through using the fog to pass undetected onto the height. Here they established HMG positions to fire on 3. and 5./Gebirgsjäger-Regiment 139. Stautner ordered the last HMG with 2 Zug of Kompanie Müller onto Litlebalak. Two platoons from 2./Gebirgsjäger-Regiment 139 with a heavy mortar followed.

Stautner set up an HQ between heights 572 and 482. He went to see what was going on himself. A bombardment was witnessed and when it stopped, Stautner decided to storm the north peak. French 75mm guns had fired on Litlebalak, thinking the Germans were still on the height. The 30 men he was with hesitated. Stautner grabbed a grenade, stood up and shouted, 'If you want your commander killed, just lie there'. Then straightaway he charged, and his men, with loud cries, followed. They raced through the rock-strewn plateau. Stautner set up an MG himself, despite being fired at from height 648. Litlebalak was stormed and the Norwegians retreated, leaving two HMGs and other equipment. The position was reinforced with German HMGs and the 81mm mortar, later used to break up Norwegian

HMS *Ark Royal* in 1939, with a Fairey Swordfish aircraft taking off as another approaches from astern. Nos 816 and 818 RNAS squadrons flew from *Furious* until 26 April 1940, when it was decided the ship needed to go home for maintenance. From 6 May, *Ark Royal* flew 803 and 801 RNAS squadrons targeting German bombers. Swordfish from 810 RNAS Squadron from *Ark Royal* targeted the railway line. While German bombers could escape British fighters because they were faster and had a better climb rate, they usually had to jettison bombs to get away. When the bombers noticed the British fighters they gathered together, limiting attack options. Sometimes twin-engine Bf 110s and JU 88C Zerstorers from KG 30 would fly support, because single-engine fighters did not have the range. (PJF Military Collection/Alamy)

concentrations of men preparing to attack. By denying the height to the enemy, German soldiers served to guard the subsequent withdrawal of Stautner's men from interdiction.

The Norwegians did better on height 648 near Lake Kopparfjell, assaulted by 5./Infanterie-Regiment 16. The German platoon defending the height was wiped out and two HMGs were lost at 2330hrs. The Norwegians could not attack Kopparfjellet the next day, because fire from the position north-east of Litlebalak disrupted them. The Norwegian 2./16th Infantry Regiment captured German positions on height 794, threatening to block the Germans' escape route, so Dietl ordered a withdrawal to another line based on the Storelven Valley, Lake Jern on the Haugfjell Plateau to point 620 near the Swedish border. This was complete by the early hours of 22 May. Stautner had marched south to Haugfjell, as his position was about to be surrounded. German MG positions on height 482 stopped the enemy from seeing what was going on. Stautner then established positions south of Lake Sirkel, blocking the road. The French 14e Bataillon de Chasseurs Alpins occupied positions on the north-west side of the road and would stay there, but make no attacks.

By 13 May, the thaw had started and the melting snow ran from the hillsides. On 19 May, thick clouds of fog had seeped into the valleys and some way up the hills. Rain soaked the uniforms, snow entrenchments started to melt. Loose rock was used to build shelters. Small gullies and clefts in the rock were occupied. On 22 May, Norwegian II./16th Infantry Regiment was ordered off the plateau for a week's rest, as they had fought for nine days at the front.

KUBERG

The Norwegians had also launched I./16th Infantry Regiment on positions east of Kopparfjell. The battalion marched 17km to Bratbakken at the southern end of Raudalen on 14 May. At 0400hrs on 6 May, 1./Gebirgsjäger-Regiment 139 had marched to Kuberg from Lake Hartvik and had had plenty of time to build defences. A number of peaks were occupied, as it was anticipated that the Norwegians would employ a wide encircling manoeuvre. Foggy weather with frequent snow showers aided the Norwegians' approach on these positions. On 14 May, Feldwebel Bussmer's 28-man Ski Zug was located on the Naeverfjell at 935m and defended the summit from sustained Norwegian attacks. When the HMG ammunition was used up, the Germans departed. The following morning the Norwegian 2./16th Infantry Regiment took 18 men from the platoon prisoner. The Norwegians occupied the valley and on 16 May approached height 794. Trautner's 14-man platoon with a single HMG was sent to the endangered peak. Also that day Leutnant Becker with part of 1./Fallschirmjäger-Regiment 1 had parachuted onto Bjørnfjell. Dietl told them to march on Kuberg. Two HMGs from Becker's force were placed on point 794 with the rest situated close by.

On the morning of 16 May, the Norwegian 2./16th Infantry Regiment assaulted the Kuberg and height 794, making use of boulders and crevasses that existed on the high plateau. From the high peaks, the Norwegians dominated the approaches, targeting the German positions with mortars

GERMAN

A. III./Gebirgsjäger-Regiment 139
B. 13./Gebirgsjäger-Regiment 139 (less elements)
C. Ski Zug Trautner
D. Ski Zug Bussmer
E. 1./Fallschirmjäger-Regiment 1, HMG Zug (less elements)
F. I./Gebirgsjäger-Regiment 139 (less elements)
G. 2 Zug, Kompanie Müller
H. 1./Gebirgsjäger-Regiment 139
I. 2./Gebirgsjäger-Regiment 139 (less elements)
J. 1./Fallschirmjäger-Regiment 1 (less elements)

DAHL

Alta

LOKEN

6

BUKKEDALEN

KOPPARFJELLET

LAKE KOPPERFJELL

LITLEBALAK

LITLEBALAK AND KOPPERFJELL, 14–22 MAY 1940

Shown here is the German defence of Litlebalak and Kopperfjell as the Norwegians attack.

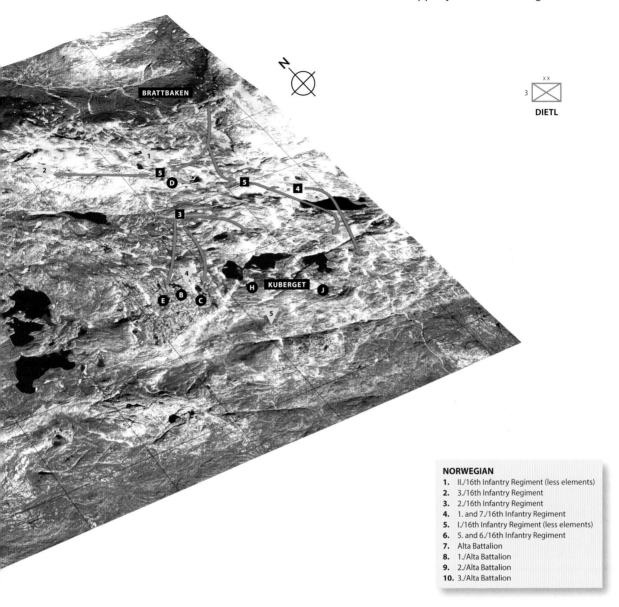

▼ EVENTS

1. Morning, 14 May: Norwegian 1st Platoon from 7./16th Infantry Regiment captures height 875.

2. Afternoon, 14 May: 2./16th Infantry Regiment attacks Ski Zug Bussmer on height 935. The following morning most of the ski platoon is captured whilst trying to escape.

3. 14–18 May: II./16th Infantry Regiment has started its attack on 14 May from Bukkedalen on the height of Kopperfjell. From height 717, 5th plus 6th companies attack on both sides of Lake Kopperfjell supported by HMGs and mortars on 17 May. Progress is slow, as is the attack by 3rd and 6th companies on Kopperfjellet. A snow storm ends the attack.

4. 16–17 May: 2./16th Infantry Regiment attacks height 794 establishing positions on it. On 17 May, Leutnant Müller, counter-attacking with 50 men from 13./Gebirgsjäger-Regiment 139, is killed on the height.

5. 16–17 May: On Kuberget, 7./16th Infantry Regiment attacks, followed by 1st Company. German defences on the height hold.

6. 20 May: The Alta Battalion attacks Litlebalak, capturing the height. Stautner with 2 Zug, Kompanie Müller successfully counter-attacks. 2./Gebirgsjäger-Regiment 139 establishes mortars and HMGs on the height.

7. 20 May: Height 648 near Lake Kopperfjell is stormed by 5./16th Infantry Regiment. The Germans lose 50 men.

8. 22 May: German positions on Kuberget and Kopperfjellet are no longer able to hold with height 794 captured. Dietl orders a deployment to the Jern lakes and the Haugfjellet. German positions on height 482 near Litlebalak prevent the Norwegians from noticing what is going on.

Luftwaffe bombers from KG 26 and KG 100 were active over Narvik against Allied shipping. On 16 May, a bomb from a He 111 hit *Resolution*; two days later, the ship was sent to Scapa Flow. In the early morning of 23 May, the destroyer *Fame* was looking at beaches off Orneset and when patrolling around Rombaksfjord was nearly hit by a bomb from a plane. Steering on the port side was put out of action. The Germans would not be able to carry all the operations they wanted, because a sufficient fuel supply to Trondheim to meet all demands was not guaranteed. When British fighters started to operate from Bardufoss, German losses of Heinkels, like the destroyed aircraft shown here, started to increase. (Arkiv i Nordland, CC BY-SA 2.0)

and MGs. By 2200hrs, height 794 was surrounded. Trautner was killed defending the position as the Norwegians closed in. Two of his men were also killed, and five taken prisoner, including three wounded. Oberfeldwebel Rohr took command. Reinforced by groups of Fallschirmjäger sent to boost his numbers, he counter-attacked. The Norwegians were thrown back. On the morning of 17 May, 13./Gebirgsjäger-Regiment 139 with 50 men, commanded by Leutnant Müller, joined Rohr and counter-attacked, trying to get to the peak. Müller with five of his men would be shot by snipers. The peak was lost again when the Norwegians attacked. Yet despite the Norwegian 7./16th Infantry Regiment and then Norwegian 1./16th Infantry Regiment attacking German positions on the eastern side of Kuberg, German positions held. However, from 15 to 17 May, 1./Gebirgsjäger-Regiment 139 experienced 72 casualties, so Dietl ordered them off the position to concentrate on Bjørnfjell.

Reinforcements were needed and soon arrived. At 1500hrs on 17 May, 3./Gebirgsjäger-Regiment 138 reached point 620 from positions at Lake Jern. At 0100hrs on 19 May, 74 men from the Fallschirmjäger-Regiment 1, commanded by Leutnant Mosinger, arrived on Kuberg. Sailors from Marine-Kompanie Erdmenger were sent, too. Marine-Kompanie Steinecker and Marine-Kompanie Weinlich deployed on Rundfjeldet and Haugfjell, respectively. On 19 May, Steinecker deployed to point 620. Gruppe von Schleebrugge was formed to command the forces on the Kuberg to the Swedish border. The 1./Fallschirmjäger-Regiment 1 occupied the Kuberg main position with 1./Gebirgsjäger-Regiment 139 held as the reserve for the group. Ski Zug Rohr was the reserve for the Kuberg. Late on 22 May, the Germans retreated from Kuberg, unseen in thick fog.

THE ORNESET LANDING AND BEISFJORD, 28 MAY 1940

By late May, Major Haussels, who commanded the Narvik garrison, had Marine-Kompanie von Dienst with Marine-Kompanie Freytag on the right around Tunnel 3. The German naval Artillery Section, commanded by Oberleutnant Noller, was at Orneset. Next to them was 6./Gebirgsjäger-Regiment 139 and Haussels' Pionier-Zug on the Framnes Peninsula. Two other naval companies occupied the harbour area. Meanwhile, 1./Gebirgsjäger-Regiment 137, 108 men with an MMG and medium mortar commanded by Oberleutnant Schweiger, was positioned between Tunnels 3 and 4. Most companies had 70 men with six LMGs. Freytag additionally had two 3.7cm guns and one MMG, 6./Gebirgsjäger-Regiment 139 two MMGs, and the two naval companies by the harbour area had two Norwegian HMGs each. On the Framnes Peninsula, three medium mortars and two infantry guns covered the northern coast. Haussels had his HMG platoon from 10./Gebirgsjäger-Regiment 139 on the slopes overlooking the town, with four covering the harbour and two on the Fagernesfjell to support 8./Gebirgsjäger-Regiment 139, which was on the other side of Beisfjord. Two mountain guns stood 750m north-east of the railway station. A 3.7cm gun and seven 2cm guns were positioned to protect against enemy landings and planes. Haussels had nearly 1,000 men, including 450 Gebirgsjäger. The tunnels were good defence positions, guarding men from the effects of the bombardment and forcing the Allies to attack on a narrow front.

Béthouart argued that an evacuation was not feasible if the Germans retained possession of the town. On 24 May, Cork had got the order to prepare to withdraw from northern Norway. The continuation of the attack would suggest to the Germans that the Allies had no such intention. At the same time as the landing at Orneset, the Poles would attack the Germans from Beisfjord and British destroyers from Rombaksfjord would target tunnel hideouts along the railway. *Southampton* would bombard positions by Beisfjord. *Cairo* with *Coventry*, *Firedrake* and *Beagle* would focus on targets around the town and harbour. The commanders were on board *Cairo*. The sloop *Stork* would be sailing by the landing craft to look out for enemy aircraft. Fighters from Bardufoss would fly air cover. Guns from a Norwegian battery and two French 75mm batteries would support the landing from Øyjord. A French battery and two 25pdrs would support Polish I., II. and IV./Independent Highland Brigade. The other Polish battalion stayed at Ballangen.

Late on 27 May, the British fleet could be seen sailing along Ofotfjord. Aircraft from *Glorious* circled above the town and four destroyers entered Rombaksfjord with transports lying in wait by Herjangsfjord. The bombardment soon began, targeting Framnes Peninsula, Fagernesfjell, the railway and the shores of Ankenes. Shells split the rock, sending fragments flying asunder. Artillery batteries targeted the town, especially the railway station. The coast east of Tarneset and Taraldsvik was particularly prioritized and was soon enveloped in a thick cloud of gunpowder and detritus. Ten boats could be seen rounding the headland at Orneset and motoring along the shoreline with the first part of the French I./13e Demi-Brigade de Légion Étrangère, 290 soldiers, to unload once they got to the bay at 0030hrs. The soldiers from the French Légion Étrangère embarked on two LCMs and three LCAs landed on the beach at Orneset.

ORNESET PLATEAU, 28 MAY 1940 (PP. 60–61)

The French I./13e Demi-Brigade de Légion Étrangère troops were first onto the Orneset beach with orders to occupy Tunnel 1 at Orneshaugen, 100m up the slope. The tunnel roof was 70m wide, and if the attack was to continue the soldiers would be using this roof. A further 200m onwards and higher up was a plateau, a 150m-long ridge with a marsh below the crest, which was hidden from Rombaksfjord below. The troops of I./13e Demi-Brigade de Légion Étrangère (**1**) were ordered to wait there until relieved by the Norwegians of Major Hyldmo's II./15th Infantry Regiment (**2**).

When they all got to the plateau by about 0430hrs (already in full daylight), Oberleutnant Schweiger's counter-attack started (**3**). MGs and mortars were used on the Norwegians and French gathered there. Soon the Germans approached with SMGs and grenades. The commander of 7./15th Infantry Regiment, Captain Haerland (**4**, armed with a Norwegian/Kongsberg colt pistol, and with his rank indicated by the three pips on his collar), recalled a German with a grenade jumping up 20–30m away from him. The grenade whirled past him as he threw himself onto the ground and rolled away just in time. His company would lose eight killed and 13 wounded in the fighting.

The Norwegians shown here are in their summer uniforms, and wearing their *Finnmarkslue* service caps. The legionnaires are equipped as mountain infantry, with distinguishing helmet insignia showing a grenade (**5**). The legionnaires also wear their light-coloured *chèches* (scarves, **6**) tied around their necks.

Norwegian Second Lieutenant Gunnar Steiro with his platoon from 6./15th Infantry Regiment was brought up to help when a mortar round wounded him. He was bandaged and then continued to lead his platoon. Norwegian 2nd Platoon, 6./15th Infantry Regiment, commanded by Sergeant Larsen, helped out Norwegian 5./15th Infantry Regiment on the right by attacking the Germans from the side from high ground.

The guns of Allied ships assisted the attack with HE and smoke produced by the blast of the shells. The exploding rounds set fire to the dry forest floor, as these were hot days with temperatures of 25 degrees Celsius.

The German counter-attack failed. Oberleutnant Schweiger was killed, as were two of his platoon leaders; the other platoon leader was critically injured.

The Norwegian battalion lost 17 killed and 34 wounded. 7th Company had 25 per cent casualties. 6th Medical Company operated on 44 wounded men. Leaders of the battalion had shown they could rally the men and show by example; Haerland, for example, took a machine gun from a wounded soldier when he was shot. Norwegian-French relations were not entirely harmonious, however: Haerland described how when the battle had finished and they got to where they had placed their backpacks, they found the contents looted by French troops.

Oberleutnant Noller's 50 men, equipped with an HMG and six LMGs, could fire only a few shots, as they were mostly pinned down by the supporting gunfire from Allied artillery and destroyers. When the bombardment lifted temporarily, they then had the Allied soldiers on the beach targeting them. Noller was soon wounded and his men started to withdraw to the blockhouse by Tunnel 1. The bombardment had not let up against other positions. German Marine-Kompanie Freytag and 1./Gebirgsjäger-Regiment 137 on the right were pinned down at the ore railway and the tunnels. Haussels sent a runner to Schweiger to tell him to head immediately to Orneset with 1./Gebirgsjäger-Regiment 137. The platoon-sized Train Station Company was ordered to deploy, too. They would be supported by a section of pioneers commanded by Leutnant Fink. Only the pioneers fought with any determination; the sailors of the Train Station Company fled at the first sight of the enemy. By 0200hrs the Allies had got to the railway line. The messenger sent to Schweiger had not got through.

The French were first on the beach and had orders to occupy Tunnel 1 at Orneshaugen, 100m up the slope. The tunnel roof was 70m wide and if the attack was to continue, the soldiers would be using this roof. Further on another 200m higher up was the plateau, a 150m-long ridge with a marsh on the other side of the crest hidden from Rombaksfjord. The French I./13e Demi-Brigade de Légion Étrangère was ordered to push onto the Taraldsvikfjell summit and wait there to be relieved by the Norwegians of Major Hyldmo's II./15th Infantry Regiment. The commander of the French I./13e Demi-Brigade de Légion Étrangère was killed by shrapnel from a round fired by a German gun located by a railway tunnel when he was at Øyjord waiting with the second batch of his battalion. The round killed 10–15 legionnaires and wounded many others. The legionnaires marched further along the coast, delaying the loading operation and exposing those of French I./13e Demi-Brigade de Légion Étrangère on the landing beach.

The first Norwegian soldiers were supposed to disembark by 0130hrs from fishing boats. They would also be delayed by an hour. Initially, they would deploy two companies and an HMG platoon. The Norwegian 5./15th Infantry Regiment was ordered to the right and Norwegian 7./15th Infantry Regiment with the HMG platoon to the left. They were to clear the area to the foot of Fagersnesfjell. The Norwegian 6./15th Infantry Regiment was the reserve and would land with the second echelon of the Norwegian contingent. The HMGs and mortars from the Norwegian 8./15th Infantry Regiment would occupy positions to support them.

At 0230hrs the second landing of the Norwegians started. When this was complete, the entire French I./13e Demi-Brigade de Légion Étrangère had landed, too. The French from this second echelon from the rocks at Orneset targeted 6./Gebirgsjäger-Regiment 139's

At 0650hrs, Major Haussels issued the orders to evacuate Narvik. Baggage and equipment was to be abandoned. The munitions depot was destroyed. Three mortars and two light infantry guns were disabled. The smoke and fumes of battle also helped. Some naval personnel on Framnes did not receive the order and would be surrounded. Here, both Norwegian and French personnel are seen on the road to town surrounded by the debris of the German hasty retreat. (Arkiv i Nordland, CC BY-SA 2.0)

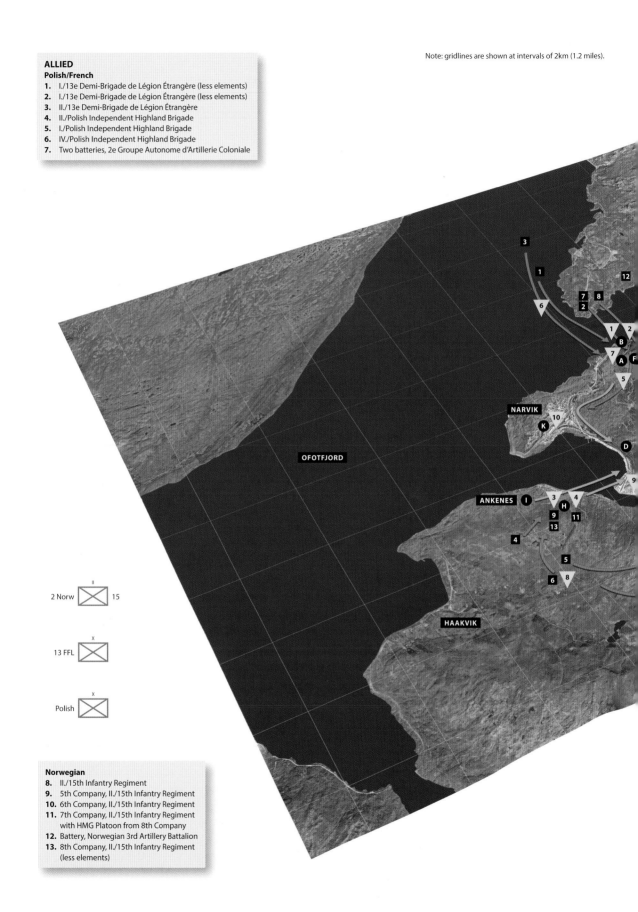

Note: gridlines are shown at intervals of 2km (1.2 miles).

ALLIED
Polish/French
1. I./13e Demi-Brigade de Légion Étrangère (less elements)
2. I./13e Demi-Brigade de Légion Étrangère (less elements)
3. II./13e Demi-Brigade de Légion Étrangère
4. II./Polish Independent Highland Brigade
5. I./Polish Independent Highland Brigade
6. IV./Polish Independent Highland Brigade
7. Two batteries, 2e Groupe Autonome d'Artillerie Coloniale

2 Norw ⫇ 15

13 FFL ⫇

Polish ⫇

OFOTFJORD

NARVIK

ANKENES

HAAKVIK

Norwegian
8. II./15th Infantry Regiment
9. 5th Company, II./15th Infantry Regiment
10. 6th Company, II./15th Infantry Regiment
11. 7th Company, II./15th Infantry Regiment
    with HMG Platoon from 8th Company
12. Battery, Norwegian 3rd Artillery Battalion
13. 8th Company, II./15th Infantry Regiment
    (less elements)

ASSAULT ON ORNESET AND BEISFJORD, 28 MAY 1940

Shown here are the Allied landings at Orneset and the Polish attack on Beisfjord.

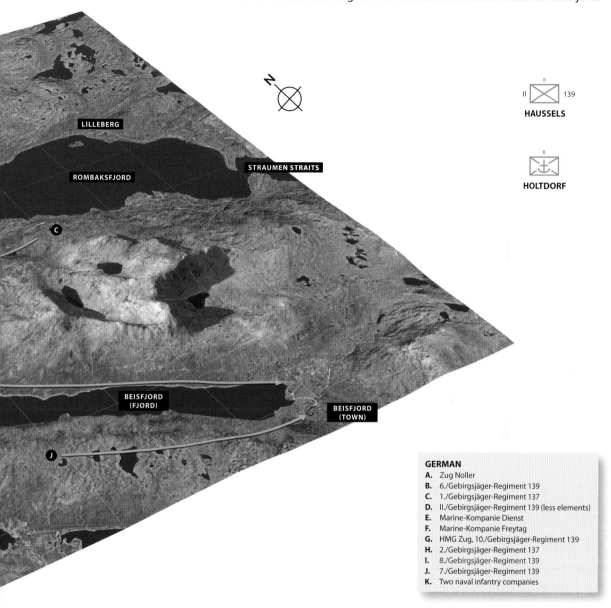

LILLEBERG

ROMBAKSFJORD

STRAUMEN STRAITS

C

BEISFJORD (FJORD)

BEISFJORD (TOWN)

J

HAUSSELS — II ⊠ 139

HOLTDORF

GERMAN

A. Zug Noller
B. 6./Gebirgsjäger-Regiment 139
C. 1./Gebirgsjäger-Regiment 137
D. II./Gebirgsjäger-Regiment 139 (less elements)
E. Marine-Kompanie Dienst
F. Marine-Kompanie Freytag
G. HMG Zug, 10./Gebirgsjäger-Regiment 139
H. 2./Gebirgsjäger-Regiment 137
I. 8./Gebirgsjäger-Regiment 139
J. 7./Gebirgsjäger-Regiment 139
K. Two naval infantry companies

▼ EVENTS

1. 0015hrs: Following a 35-minute bombardment, 290 men of I./13e Demi-Brigade de Légion Étrangère land at Orneset. They march on Tunnel 1.

2. 0230hrs: Second part of I./13e Demi-Brigade de Légion Étrangère with II./15th Infantry Regiment land at Orneset. The Norwegians start to climb to the plateau above Tunnel 1.

3. 0300hrs: Following a bombardment, Polish troops attack 8./Gebirgsjäger-Regiment 139 near Ankenes.

4. 0330hrs: Riegler with 2./Gebirgsjäger-Regiment 137 counter-attacks the Poles. Whilst successful, he is wounded and made prisoner along with many of his men.

5. 0430hrs: The Norwegians reach the French on the plateau at the same time as the Germans launch a counter-attack with 1./Gebirgsjäger-Regiment 137. The Norwegians, with the support of destroyers firing from the fjord, repel the counter-attack.

6. 0445hrs: German aircraft target the fleet. The command ship *Cairo* is damaged.

7. 0615hrs: II./13e Demi-Brigade de Légion Étrangère lands at Taraldsvik Bay following a bombardment lasting an hour.

8. 0700–2045hrs: I./Polish Independent Highland Brigade attacks 7./Gebirgsjäger-Regiment 139. Dietl sends Marine-Kompanie Clemens with platoons of Fallschirmjäger-Regiment 1 commanded by Leutnant Keuchal to establish a frontline near Beisfjord. 7./Gebirgsjäger-Regiment 139 withdraws to Beisfjord at 2045hrs.

9. 0650–2030hrs: At 0650hrs, Haussels orders the evacuation of Narvik. HMGs of 10./Gebirgsjäger-Regiment 139 plus 6./Gebirgsjäger-Regiment 139 hold firm whilst the garrison uses the road to Beisfjord from Fagernes.

10. Late afternoon: 7./15th Infantry Regiment gets to Taraldsvikfjell. The town is liberated by 5. and 6./15th Infantry Regiment.

positions at Taraldsvik. The German HMG platoon leader on Fagernesfjell had seen the French approach Taraldsvik and decided to send two HMGs to stop them at the railway. This they succeeded in doing, though when the French started to climb the Taraldviksfjell again the German machine gunners were ambushed by enemy forces concealed in a birch wood. Those that survived were taken prisoner. Elsewhere, near Tunnel 1, Leutnant Siebt, with a motley collection of men, stalled the French Légion Étrangère; his men destroyed the tunnel when he went missing at 0400hrs. The German mountain guns engaged enemy batteries until 0330hrs, when ammunition was depleted.

The Norwegians had loaded a platoon from the Norwegian 6./15th Infantry Regiment onto the first echelon boats and this platoon was the first to reach French elements on the plateau using the tunnel roof, followed by 5./15th Infantry Regiment and 7./15th Infantry Regiment. The going was tough, as extra ammunition was being hauled up the steep slope to the plateau. When they got to the plateau by about 0430hrs, the German counter-attack, led by Oberleutnant Schweiger, started. Machine guns and mortars were used on the Norwegians and French gathered there.

Between 0400hrs and 0500hrs, the British bombardment intensified. At 0615hrs, another landing took place with tanks in support, this time at Taraldsvik Bay. German aircraft had delayed this landing by attacking the fleet at 0445hrs. He 111s approached the command ship at 6,000ft. The first 50kg bomb that hit struck the closed ammunition supply of the pom-pom gun deck. The others exploded on the deck between the funnels. The commanders had a near miss. Despite this, the men who disembarked, the French II./13e Demi-Brigade de Légion Étrangère, threatened to encircle the town by marching on Fagernes. Major Haussels started to realize that the road along Beisfjord was his only way out. Meanwhile, Schweiger had not received any orders to counter-attack. On his own initiative, he decided to attack the enemy landings. Organizing this among the British bombardment delayed his approach somewhat and not until 0700hrs, according to Buchner, could the attack start; the aim was to move on the slopes of the Taraldsfjell that were above Tunnel 1. He met with some success until British destroyers noticed him and used light guns on his force. Schweiger was killed, as were two naval officers. Leutnant Enzinger, the artillery commander, was wounded. Buchner does not mention the importance of the Norwegians to Schweiger's defeat. They had ascended to the plateau and from there they were counter-attacked by the Germans, according to Norwegian sources at the earlier time of 0430hrs.

Polish troops pause to eat their rations by the roadside after landing in the port of Harstad. (© Imperial War Museum, HU 128126)

6./Gebirgsjäger-Regiment 139 and the MG platoon on Fagernesfjell covered the move of the garrison when Haussels ordered the evacuation, firing onto the harbour road. On the Ankenes Peninsula, German 8./Gebirgsjäger-Regiment 139 held fast and distracted the Poles from firing on the road. Haussels got five trucks together at Fagernes and these took the men to Beisfjord. Ordered to evacuate Ankenes, 8./Gebirgsjäger-Regiment 139 and 2./Gebirgsjäger-Regiment

137 would join the retreat later in the day. Between midday and 1530hrs, Kapitanleutnant von Freytag led 70–80 men to stop further attempts by the Norwegians and French to advance on the Taraldsvikfjell; he then had orders to withdraw to Tunnel 3. Marine-Bataillon Holtdorf at 1400hrs urgently asked for reinforcements. Dietl only sent a section and told them to hold Tunnel 3. The French did not arrive there until 2045hrs.

Earlier, the British bombardment had also targeted Ankenes, setting fire to 30 houses there and Nyborg nearby where 2./Gebirgsjäger-Regiment 137 was held ready. At 0200hrs, the Poles attacked 8./Gebirgsjäger-Regiment 139's positions. Naval personnel attached to them started to flee. At 0230hrs, 2./Gebirgsjäger-Regiment 137 with two platoons deployed to help. Oberleutnant Riegler launched a counter-attack; with only 15 men, he was so successful that he occupied the Polish command post on point 295. However, he was soon wounded and captured. Most of his men were taken prisoner. On the Ankenes road, a platoon of tanks advanced with accompanying infantry from the Polish 2./Independent Highland Brigade on a German platoon comprising 47 sailors and nine *Gebirgsjäger* with a light AT gun crewed by five men. A minefield immobilized the first tank and the others could not get past. The escorting infantry experienced withering fire. By 0545hrs though, 2./Gebirgsjäger-Regiment 137 had to retreat and by late morning, they had started to row to Fagernes. The last of the Germans on the peninsula would only make the journey by 1700hrs. Some of them were shot at by Poles and boats sunk, forcing the occupants to swim. Located on the peaks to the east, 7./Gebirgsjäger-Regiment 139 would also be targeted. Poles attempted to surround point 606. Meanwhile, points 773 and 650 were attacked too. Polish mortars succeeded in destroying some HMG positions. At 0600hrs, a co-ordinated attack by 1,000 men of the Polish I./Independent Highland Brigade started. The southern front began to crumble. Dietl sent Marine-Kompanie Clemens with two platoons of *Fallschirmjäger* commanded by Leutnant Keuchal to the Lakselven Valley to meet soldiers from Fagernes. These soldiers needed to make a new defence line before the Poles broke through 7./Gebirgsjäger-Regiment 139's positions.

The Polish attacks continued all day. At 1700hrs, point 606 had to be evacuated before the position was encircled. At 1945hrs, orders from the commander of 7./Gebirgsjäger-Regiment 139 to pull back to Beisfjord were received. The badly wounded were the first to arrive, by about 2000hrs. Oberfeldwebel Hausotter with an MG crew on Skavtuva held out to the last round. Once he was wounded, his men carried him to the German lines, because he did not want to be captured. Those who could escape at 0300hrs on 29 May staggered through the mountain pass on point 660 to safety.

DEFENDING THE ORE RAILWAY

Dietl told Hauptmann Walther with 3./Fallschirmjäger-Regiment 1 to command the defenders along the ore railway. Communications were lacking and Walther would not be able to talk with Haussels. Point 1,436 was not occupied and Dietl ordered Walther to retreat to the Straumen Straits. The Allies struck the southern front hard on 30 May. A wide sweep took them to Lake Sildvik, threatening to cut off Walther's command on

Sildvik and Haugfjell, 29 May–10 June 1940

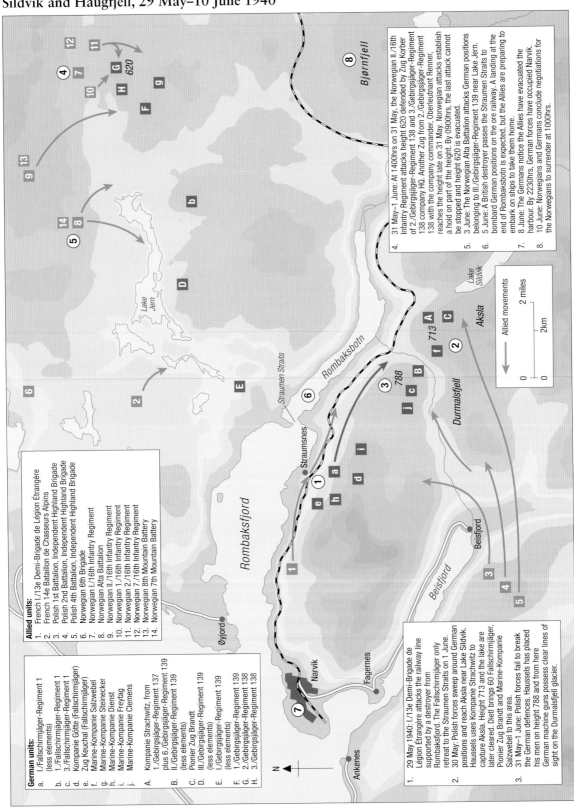

German units:

a. I./Fallschirmjäger-Regiment 1 (less elements)
b. 1./Fallschirmjäger-Regiment 1
c. 3./Fallschirmjäger-Regiment 1
d. Kompanie Götte (Fallschirmjäger)
e. Zug Keuchal (Fallschirmjäger)
f. Marine-Kompanie Salzwedel
g. Marine-Kompanie Steinecker
h. Marine-Kompanie Dienst
i. Marine-Kompanie Freytag
j. Marine-Kompanie Clemens

A. Kompanie Strachwitz, from
1./Gebirgsjäger-Regiment 137
plus 6./Gebirgsjäger-Regiment 139
B. II./Gebirgsjäger-Regiment 139 (less elements)
C. Pionier Zug Brandt
D. III./Gebirgsjäger-Regiment 139 (less elements)
E. I./Gebirgsjäger-Regiment 139 (less elements)
F. 1./Gebirgsjäger-Regiment 139
G. 2./Gebirgsjäger-Regiment 138
H. 3./Gebirgsjäger-Regiment 138

Allied units:

1. French I./13e Demi-Brigade de Légion Étrangère (less elements)
2. French 14e Bataillon de Chasseurs Alpins
3. Polish 1st Battalion, Independent Highland Brigade
4. Polish 2nd Battalion, Independent Highland Brigade
5. Polish 4th Battalion, Independent Highland Brigade
6. Norwegian 6th Brigade
7. Norwegian I./16th Infantry Regiment
8. Norwegian Alta Battalion
9. Norwegian II./16th Infantry Regiment
10. Norwegian 1./16th Infantry Regiment
11. Norwegian 2./16th Infantry Regiment
12. Norwegian 7./16th Infantry Regiment
13. Norwegian 8th Mountain Battery
14. Norwegian 7th Mountain Battery

1. 29 May 1940: I./13e Demi-Brigade de Légion Étrangère attacks the railway line supported by a destroyer from Rombaksfjord. The Fallschirmjäger only retreat to the Straumen Straits on 1 June.

2. 30 May: Polish forces sweep around German positions and reach Aksla near Lake Sildvik. Haussels uses Kompanie Strachwitz to capture Aksla. Height 713 and the lake are later cleared. Dietl brings 60 Fallschirmjäger, Pionier Zug Brandt and Marine-Kompanie Salzwebel to this area.

3. 31 May–1 June: Polish forces fail to break the German defences. Haussels has placed his men on height 788 and from here German machine guns possess clear lines of sight on the Durmalsfjell glacier.

4. 31 May–1 June: At 1400hrs on 31 May, the Norwegian II./16th Infantry Regiment attacks height 620 defended by Zug Körber of 2./Gebirgsjäger-Regiment 138 and 3./Gebirgsjäger-Regiment 138 company HQ. Another Zug from 2./Gebirgsjäger-Regiment 138 with the company commander, Oberleutnant Renner, reaches the height late on 31 May. Norwegian attacks establish a hold on part of the height. By 0900hrs, the last attack cannot be stopped and height 620 is evacuated.

5. 3 June: The Norwegian Alta Battalion attacks German positions belonging to III./Gebirgsjäger-Regiment 139 near Lake Jern.

6. 5 June: A British destroyer passes the Straumen Straits to bombard German positions on the ore railway. A landing at the end of Rombaksbotn is expected, but the Allies are preparing to embark on ships to take them home.

7. 8 June: The Germans notice the Allies have evacuated the harbour. By 2230hrs, German forces have occupied Narvik.

8. 10 June: Norwegians and Germans conclude negotiations for the Norwegians to surrender at 1000hrs.

Allied movements

0 2km
0 2 miles

N

the ore railway. Haussels noticed that Kompanie Strachwitz was being sent back to Dietl by Walther, as enemy attacks on the ore railway had dissipated. He used them to counter-attack the Poles on Aksla. Dietl personally took Pionier-Zug Brandt, 60 Fallschirmjäger commanded by Leutnant Rottke and Marine-Kompanie Salzwebel to point 713 to clear the Poles from the lake. These were the last of the reserves. The Poles decided that they were vulnerable and decided to pull back. A more determined Polish attack the next day met stronger defences when they pushed through the Molnelven Valley. On 1 June, another German retreat to the steep cliffs of the Sildvikfjell (point 788) was made. Haussels placed MG positions on the peak and from there Durmalsfjell glacier could be swept with fire.

On 29 May, Walther on the ore railway had an easier time, as the French were not hurrying to attack. They waited until 1720hrs, when a British destroyer from Rombaksfjord bombarded Tunnel 4. The retreat to the Straumen Straits occurred on 30 May and the next day the French attacked the railway without success. Walther had about 200 *Fallschirmjäger* and 250 sailors. The clear weather spell brought *Luftwaffe* support, especially on 2 June. Ammunition was scarce and Dietl was happy that the enemy only conducted isolated attacks. No aerial supplies could get to them on 3 June when the weather turned. Destroyers roamed freely along Rombaksfjord, bombarding the positions of Walther's men. The Germans expected a landing at the end of the fjord, thus isolating Walther and Haussels from the rest of Dietl's command.

POINT 620 AND HAUGFJELL

The III./Gebirgsjäger-Regiment 139 looked out onto the Straumen Straits and had a Gebirgsjäger company in reserve. I./Gebirgsjäger-Regiment 139 was on the slopes of Haugfeldet with four HMGs, four mortars and 12 LMGs. The surfaces of the lakes were melting and this made a good barrier against enemy attacks. German positions still had to be established among the broad snowfields of the mountains, where there were no trees or brush. Cloud and fog created wet conditions. Norwegian soldiers gradually occupied the peaks facing the Germans. On 27 May, the Norwegians attacked the front at Lake Jern and suffered heavy losses. They deployed forces on the German right to break through to the Swedish border.

Norwegian soldiers on the frontline north of Narvik. Supply lines were stretched with men hauling packs weighing 35kg through snow and onto hilltops at 800m. Seeing the Germans strengthen positions led many to question why they were not still attacking. Only on 29 May would the Norwegian I./16th Infantry Regiment be dispatched to attack hill 620 near the Swedish border. (Matteo Omied/Alamy)

LEUTNANT BUJNOCH'S PLATOON DEFEND HEIGHT 620 (PP. 70–71)

The Norwegians targeted height 620 on the morning of 31 May, once they had closed to within range of infantry weapons the previous day. The weather changed to sleet and slush. With fog concealing the approach, two platoons of the Norwegian 1./16th Infantry Regiment attacked point 620, which was being defended by Oberleutnant Polder's HQ section and Zug Korber from 2./Gebirgsjäger Regiment 138, equipped with an HMG and an 81mm mortar. Norwegian HMGs and mortars dominated the position from point 1,067.

When patches of fog appeared, the Norwegian platoons from a nearby height closed to grenade-throwing range without being shot at. They were only 20–30m from the German positions when combat began. Grenades that the Germans threw went past the Norwegians, because they had approached so close. The Norwegians managed to entrench on the peak.

The I./16th Infantry Regiment would deploy two companies to the attack on height 620 supported by HMGs and mortars. Captain Gunnar Elstad of 2./16th Infantry Regiment proposed assaulting the plateau to the east of height 620, but had to get the battalion commander to agree to the proposal, and this put the attack off until the next day. This enabled the Germans to send reinforcements to the height.

By 1900hrs Oberleutnant Renner had taken command on height 620. Korber had used his last medium mortar rounds. The HMG gunner and loader were wounded. They were on positions on the other side of the crest from the Norwegians. Positions could not be dug because of the stone under foot. At 2200hrs, following HMG and mortar fire targeting them, the Norwegians attacked. The German light mortar then fired its last rounds at 2300hrs.

The German crew went to get ammunition; this was a ten-hour round trip. By the end of the day, Renner's 2nd Platoon had arrived, comprising 30 men commanded by Leutnant Bujnoch, bringing badly needed light mortar rounds and grenades.

At 0600hrs the following morning, the Norwegians resorted to heavy shelling. Entrenching on the rocky surface was not possible. From the higher ridge opposite, the Norwegians, with good lines of sight, plastered the hill with fire. 2nd Company then moved forward again with 100 men at 0745hrs. Bujnoch's platoon from positions located on small hillocks covered Korber's platoon.

This scene depicts Gebirgsjäger from Leutnant Bujnoch's platoon located on a small hillock close to and to the south of height 620. They are targeting Norwegians who are about to attack Korber's platoon from the side of the height. Norwegian mortar rounds are exploding to the front of Bujnoch's positions. Bujnoch (**1**) is wearing a wind jacket (*Windbluse*, **2**) and is firing his MP 40 (**3**). On his belt are a pouch for the MP 40 magazines (**4**), a pistol holster (**5**) and a map case (**6**). He is wearing gloves to protect him from the cold, and the distinctive *Bergmütze* cap (**7**) with a metal edelweiss badge attached to the left side of the cap's curtain. Bujnoch's men wear a mixture of wind jackets and great coats, with gloves. One is armed with a Gewehr 33/40 rifle used by the Gebirgsjäger (**8**), while another (wearing a snow-camouflage helmet cover) fires his MG 34 (**9**). Another is pulling the pull cord on his Stielhandgranate (**10**), which runs from the detonator down the length of the hollow handle, emerging from the base. The Gebirgsjäger with the rifle is holding a replacement MG 34 drum magazine (**11**) for the machine gunner.

The border area was the responsibility of the German von Schleebrugge-Gruppe and he deployed a *Fallschirmjäger* company with four HMGs on both sides of point 456, adjoining III./Gebirgsjäger-Regiment 139, 1./Gebirgsjäger-Regiment 139 with an HMG and 81mm mortar on point 625, and Marine-Kompanie Steinecker on point 620. Windisch added Oberleutnant Polder's 3./Gebirgsjäger-Regiment 138 to Schleebrugge's force and they replaced Steinecker's Marine-Kompanie that had been moved to Rundfjeldet out of harm's way. Oberleutnant Renner's 2./Gebirgsjäger-Regiment 138 had landed between 22 and 24 May, some by flying boat, some by air. His 82 men on 25 May were told to occupy the area between I. and III./Gebirgsjäger-Regiment 139. On 29 May, Kompanie Renner was told to join von Schleebrugge-Gruppe. Renner went onto point 620 late on 31 May.

Norwegian soldiers operating a Colt M/29 HMG on the front-line north of Narvik. Captain Gunnar Elstad's 2./16th Infantry Regiment forward platoon leader had thought it was useless to attack if 1./16th Infantry Regiment's attack had not succeeded. Elstad went to 1./16th Infantry Regiment HQ when its two platoons were pinned on the slopes of height 620 to propose assaulting the plateau to the east of the height. Faller rejected this approach and wanted to use HMGs to engage the defenders when they showed themselves. Elstad had to get the battalion commander to agree to his proposal and this put the attack off until the next day. This enabled the Germans to send reinforcements to the height. (Matteo Omied/Alamy)

The Norwegians targeted point 620 on 31 May during the morning, once they had closed to within range of infantry weapons the previous day. The weather changed to sleet and slush. With fog concealing the approach, two platoons of the Norwegian 1./16th Infantry Regiment attacked point 620, which was defended by Oberleutnant Polder's HQ section and Zug Korber from 2./Gebirgsjäger-Regiment 138, equipped with an HMG and 81mm mortar. Norwegian HMGs and mortars dominated the position from point 1,067. This fire wounded Polder. Air support also helped the Norwegians.

When patches of fog appeared, the Norwegian platoons from a nearby height closed to grenade-throwing range without being shot at. They were only 20–30m from German positions when combat began. Grenades the Germans threw went past them, because they had got close. They managed to entrench on the peak. Lieutenant I. Dahlberg, commanding the Norwegian 2nd Platoon of 1./16th Infantry Regiment, used his pistol leading from the front. Meanwhile, the Norwegian 4./16th Infantry Regiment with HMGs and the two mortars could not target the Germans because of the fog. Norwegian snipers 300m from the German positions found it hard to locate them. The company commander, Captain Einar Faller, would not command from the front and Dahlberg found himself taking on that role. The I./16th Infantry Regiment would then deploy two companies to the attack on height 620, supported by HMGs and mortars. A mountain gun was also deployed, though the gunners would not use it, as the Germans were close to friendly forces.

By 1900hrs, Oberleutnant Renner was on height 620. Korber had used his last medium mortar rounds. The HMG gunner and loader were wounded. They were on positions on the other side of the crest. Positions could not be dug because of the stony terrain. At 2200hrs, after German HMG and mortar fire targeted height 620, the Norwegians attacked. The light mortar then fired its last rounds at 2300hrs. Renner's crew went to get ammunition; this was a ten-hour round trip. By the end of the day, Renner's 2nd Platoon, 30 men commanded by Leutnant Bujnoch, had arrived, bringing badly needed light mortar rounds and grenades.

It was good timing, as following a bombardment by six Allied aircraft, 200–250 Norwegians at 0245hrs attacked once again. The last of the German grenades thrown from positions on the back slope were used to force them back. *Gefreiter* Wieser, with only his pistol, had earlier fetched back an HMG captured by the Norwegians, which was used too. An hour later, the Norwegians attacked once again. The last of the light mortar rounds were fired, which persuaded most of the Norwegian 1st Platoon, 1./16th Infantry Regiment, to run, which threatened to break the company when 3rd Platoon leader, Norwegian Second Lieutenant Hovde, grabbed an MG and castigated his men. Mortars could do no harm when exploding nearby, because of the snow. At 0600hrs the Norwegians resorted to heavy shelling. At 0745hrs they attacked. This time, with ammunition running out, the Germans decided to vacate the hill. Six men were killed and 15 wounded. *Gefreiter* Bauer would die while being treated on Swedish territory.

BODØ

On 30 April, a company of Scots Guards was sent to Bodø to guard against the possibility of a German air landing. With a population of 5,000, Bodø was the only town of any size until Trondheim was reached. The expedition to Namsos by the British 146th Brigade supported by the French 5e Demi-Brigade de Chasseurs Alpins had ended and the decision to withdraw by sea was made without thinking of the possibility of retreating up the coast, fighting as they went. The area was thought to be inhospitable and the road impassable because of the thaw. The local Norwegian commander, Colonel Getz, had other ideas; supplies for his battalion were being brought by road from the small port at Mosjøen, 90 miles north of Namsos. A railway also ran for 130 miles and was clear of snow. On 30 April, the French deployed a company to Mosjøen, replaced a week later by the British, who sought to safeguard the approach to Narvik from German forces of Gebirgsjäger-Regiment 138 safely ensconced at Trondheim.

By 9 May, Colonel Gubbins with two British Independent Companies (4 and 5) had landed at Mosjøen. On 4 May, the British No. 1 Independent Company had landed at Mo, 54 miles by road from Mosjøen, and the British No. 2 Independent Company, closely followed by British No. 3 Independent Company, had landed at Bodø. On 10 May, Lieutenant-Colonel Nummendal had placed most of the reserve battalion of the Norwegian 14th Infantry Regiment at Mo. However, leadership was lacking, because many of the officers were located elsewhere. There was no battalion commander and only a single company commander. The Norwegian 2nd Company of the I./14th Infantry Regiment was already there.

This map shows the approach the Germans needed to use to get to the snow plateau. British attempts to block them would be focussed near Mo where, from 17 to 18 May, the Scots Guards held Oberstleutnant Sorko's II./Gebirgsjäger-Regiment 137. The British then quickly went through the snow plateau and got to the Irish Guards' positions at Pothus by 25 May. (Antiqua Print Gallery/Alamy)

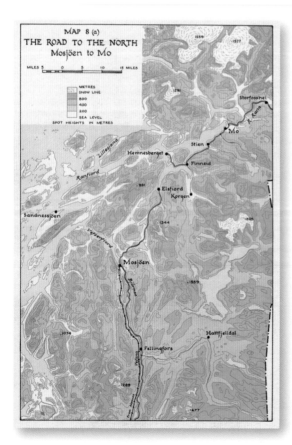

The rest of the battalion was at Mosjøen. A reserve company was at Korgen.

Gubbins found the Norwegian battalion, 400 men of I./14th Infantry Regiment, at Fellingfors, 24 miles south of Mosjøen. Germans advancing from Grong on 4 May had encountered them there, throwing them back. Gubbins brought British No. 5 Independent Company forward, supporting two Norwegian companies, ten miles to the south of Mosjøen. On 10 May, from concealed positions on the hillsides, a German column of cyclists was ambushed. Once the Germans started to deploy, Gubbins, with Norwegian support, decided he was unable to defend Mosjøen because there were no natural defence positions. He ordered British No. 1 Independent Company at Mo to safeguard the Ranfjord and wanted to make any German approach to Mo as difficult as possible. He was unaware that Germans had embarked on a steamer at Trondheim and were approaching Hemnes.

Generalleutnant Feuerstein's German 2.Gebirgs-Division was brought from Germany to assist Dietl; the land route to Trondheim from Oslo would take time and some soldiers went by plane, notably II./Gebirgsjäger-Regiment 137. On 2 May, a goods train took them to some barracks. A blown-up bridge forced them to go on foot the next day until they found some horses and open wagons and, with them, they reached Steinkjer. On 4 May, the march continued; on 5 May, they went to Grong by train. Buses took some of them onwards the next day, the rest travelled by rail. A wagon full of stones was attached to the front of the locomotive, as some of the bridges were known to be rigged with explosives set off by pressure fuses. When they got to Brekkvasselv they had to continue on foot, as the railway was completely destroyed. From looted carts and horses, a baggage train was improvised to carry the backpacks.

On 27 April, 2.Gebirgs-Division departed barracks and went to Frederikshaven, arriving two days later. A decision to switch the embarkation to Copenhagen was made because a merchant ship carrying soldiers had earlier sunk when hit by a torpedo from a British submarine. Here, soldiers from 6./Gebirgsjäger-Regiment 137 are seen on the train to Copenhagen. (Arkiv i Nordland, CC BY-SA 2.0)

The 750 men of Sorko's II./Gebirgsjäger-Regiment 137 would catch planes to Trondheim on 30 April 1940. They had with them a Pionier-Zug and 4.Batterie, Gebirgs-Artillerie-Regiment 111. Three hundred men from Gebirgsjäger-Regiment 136 would also be flown from Oslo to Trondheim, where this group photo of Gebirgsjägers was probably taken. Sorko's battalion stopped off at Kristiansand on 1 May, and took off again the following day. (Arkiv i Nordland, CC BY-SA 2.0)

On 4 May, Sorko had a battalion each from Gebirgsjäger-Regiment 137 and Gebirgsjäger-Regiment 138, companies from Gebirgsjäger-Regiment 136, an engineer platoon and three gun batteries to start his attack. His men had got to Fossmoforsen, 60km north of Grong on 6 May. Fellingfors was occupied on 8 May. Between Elfsfjord and Korgen the terrain was difficult. Hauptmann Holzinger was told to lead an expedition that would capture Hemnesberg, about 20km from Mo, and seize the road junction at Finneid. Holzinger's 300-man force comprised 1./Gebirgsjäger-Regiment 138, the mortar platoon from 4./Gebirgsjäger-Regiment 138, two mountain guns and two 20mm guns. A Norwegian steamer was commandeered and German naval personnel placed on board with a gun and MGs mounted on the deck. The 500km journey through enemy seas would be hazardous. A British submarine spotted them when they departed on 8 May and Holzinger had the ship turn back. They decided to sail late the next day. Some 70 soldiers would also be airlifted to Hemnesberg to land on the fjord by flying boat.

On 7 May, the surrender of a company of Norwegians was accepted. The prisoners of war were brought to the barracks at Steinkjer. The first casualties were suffered from snipers at Svenningdal, who changed out of uniform before fleeing. Others were lost when a group sent to parley with some Norwegians who wanted to surrender was fired upon. (Gamma-Keystone via Getty Images)

The shipping line alerted the Norwegian military and the information about the ship's departure was passed to the British. Norwegian naval ships spotted the steamer on 10 May and the HQ at Harstad was informed. The cruiser *Calcutta*, 50 miles west of Skomvaer lighthouse, was eventually ordered to intercept along with the destroyer *Zulu* at Skjelford. *Calcutta* waited for two hours until the destination of the steamer was named as Mo before she got going. Then she waited for *Zulu* to escort her, but this did not occur until 1700hrs. So, the Germans entered Ranfjord unnoticed. When the German ship arrived at the quay at 1900hrs on 10 May, the British No. 1 Independent Company, commanded by Major May, was at Mo minus a platoon at Hemnesberg. Meanwhile, *Calcutta* and *Zulu* appeared by 2015hrs and sank the steamer. The British platoon that escaped had to fight through a roadblock established by the men landed by flying boat. Hauptmann Holzinger lost nine killed and 13 wounded and missing. *Generalleutnant* Feuerstein's other formations were at least 50km distant. Only on 16 May would they get to them. Holzinger, who was supplied from the air, would attack towards Finneid, capturing the settlement on 15 May.

Hemnesberg docks pictured after the fighting. Hauptmann Holzinger's men stormed ashore here, forcing the British out at close quarters. Five German and eight British soldiers were killed in the fighting, with a larger number wounded. Two German platoon leaders were wounded. (Arkiv i Nordland, CC BY-SA 2.0)

Leutnant Rudolf had flown to nearby Sund, using two Do-26 flying boats with men from 7./Gebirgsjäger-Regiment 138. Five other flying boats soon landed a total of 70 men. When a report of flying boats landing Germans near Hemnesberg was received at Mo, Norwegian Captain Ellinger and his company was sent there to intercept them. When they reached the Hemnesoy Peninsula, British No. 1 Independent Company was encountered. Ellinger found out that 400 Germans had landed. The combined force decided to guard the road north of Finneid.

Meanwhile, Norwegian Major-General Fleischer wanted to recapture Hemnesberg so his two battalions further south could escape. Major-General Ruge was disappointed that the British had evacuated Mosjeon. Gubbins' main force north of Mosjeon could no longer risk the road and had to take sea transport to Mo. Norwegian reserves at Mosjøen had already departed for Mo by sea. The Norwegian regular battalion had to march overland, leaving baggage and heavy weapons behind. By this time, British confidence in Norwegian personnel was diminishing. This is when Major-General Mackesy decided to send the Scots Guards to Mo with some 25pdrs, Bofors guns and engineers, closely followed by the Irish Guards. A road went from Mo to Sweden and there was also the airfield nearby.

At 0500hrs on 12 May, the ships carrying the Scots Guards with Brigadier Fraser back on duty were off Mo, and the men needed to be brought onto the dock by Norwegian fishing craft. The men covered seven miles that morning with baggage still unloading at Mo, while German aircraft bombed the town. No British ships were hit and no casualties were suffered – only an empty fishing boat was sunk. The cargo ship *Margot*, with 25pdr guns on board, rammed the dock. *Margot*'s captain wanted to take his ship off with the guns still on board, because he thought unloading would take some hours. In the end, gunners unloaded the equipment within 35 minutes.

Fraser soon concluded that holding Mo would not be possible, because the fleet could not guarantee an uninterrupted flow of supplies against possible bombing and strafing. The road from Mo north to Bodø climbed high into the snow line and could be patrolled by the *Luftwaffe*. German columns had already reached Elsfjord. On 14 May, British No. 1 Independent Company and the Norwegian company commanded by Captain Ellinger abandoned Finneid and marched back to Stien, where the Scots Guards' battalion was located. When German planes attacked HMS *Somali* with Brigadier Fraser on board on 15 May, the destroyer with a wounded Fraser had to steam to Scapa Flow. Gubbins was appointed commander of 24th (Guards) Brigade in his stead. The *Luftwaffe*'s presence deterred the Royal Navy from maintaining a presence nearby; this was a pity, because a destroyer patrolling the fjord would have slowed the German advance.

The Scots Guards then took positions by Stien, placing two companies on the frontline with B Company in reserve. The Scots Guards would have to fight without

A Blohm & Voss BV 138 Seedrache (Sea Dragon) trimotor flying boat at Hemnesfjord. This German plane landed on the fjord to take the light infantry guns to Korgen. It was later shot out of the sky by a British cruiser. (Arkiv i Nordland, CC BY-SA 2.0)

Elsfjord in 1940. Battalion Sorko, II./Gerbirgsjäger-Regiment, continued to Mosjøen and then Elsfjord, with only three hours' break in 24 hours, reaching the latter settlement at 1400hrs on 13 May. The path stopped at the fjord's edge. The only way forward was over the mountains. (Arkiv i Nordland, CC BY-SA 2.0)

Soldiers of the Polish Independent Highland Brigade on board a destroyer at Harstad. On 20 May, destroyers embarked most of the Irish Guards and brought them to Bodø. Fishing craft took the others and they were all brought to the Saltdalsfjord. (© Imperial War Museum, HU 109761)

the other battalions of the brigade. By the early morning of 14 May, the Irish Guards had embarked on the Polish liner *Chorbry*, destined for Bodø. They had got to the embarkation point on the afternoon of 13 May, but no thought was given to embarking them immediately. At 0830hrs, a bomb landed 300 yards from the ship prior to *Chorbry*'s departure. Another bomb load narrowly missed at 1700hrs when the ship was still stationary, waiting for orders to go. Only at 1800hrs, when staff officers from Harstad turned up, did the ship set sail after a delay of six hours. When the Irish Guards did get going, they could see that a German plane had noticed them. A destroyer and a sloop were escorting the *Chorbry*. The Irish Guards expected to land at Bodø at 0400hrs, so the commanding officer told the men to get some sleep.

At 0015hrs on 15 May, Heinkels bombed the ship. The top decks amidships near the senior officers' cabins soon started to burn. RSM Stack formed the men up as if on the parade ground on the forward section of the ship. The lifeboats could not be lowered because the power was off and the electric motors did not work. They had to wait until the escorting destroyer was alongside. The winches aft were working, so the crew lowered the boats and they started to approach the sloop. Thirty minutes later the boats had rowed to the sloop and waited for the order to embark. Some 20 men unable to make it to a boat had jumped into the sea as the fire approached. The sloop launched a boat to pick them up. The destroyer was alongside and lowered a gangway from forward of the ship. There was no hurry or sign of haste when the men in single file went on board the destroyer. The commanding officer, second in command and two of four company commanders were killed or mortally wounded. Of the other two, only one would be back in a week's time, as the other company commander was sent to the UK. The battalion commanding officer was a captain, the company commanders mostly lieutenants. There were not enough Bren guns and no 3in mortars. The light tank platoon destined for Mo was lost. The Irish Guards went back to Harstad to refit.

Then late on 17 May, the cruiser *Effingham*, carrying the South Wales Borderers, ran aground on the Faksen shoal off Bodø. Another escorting cruiser took the men off and back to Harstad. Stockwell's British No. 2 Independent Company scrounged three Bren gun carriers and some 3in mortars.

STIEN, 17–18 MAY 1940

The woods near Stien were thick, though not in leaf. A narrow strip of ground near the fjord was clear of trees. A wider 300–400-yard strip was also clear of trees on the Dalselv. Some farms and houses stood on both sides of the Dalselv with others by the road. British D Company, Scots Guards,

A view of the Ranfjord and the settlement of Mo, 18 May 1940. (Arkiv i Nordland, CC BY-SA 2.0)

on the left had an open space by the middle of the position. A small hut was the Company HQ. Most of 16th and 18th platoons had poor lines of sight, because of the woods. Positions constructed behind 17th Platoon had good lines of sight. The positions were constructed mostly by building up layers of logs and earth, because the rocky ground meant entrenchments could not be dug to any depth. That night it snowed. The men had worked all day, did not have hot food, could not light fires and did not possess any sleeping bags. The next day the weather was better. On 14 May, a German reconnaissance aircraft was seen. The Bofors hit the plane on the pilot's second pass. He was taken prisoner once he swam out of the fjord. Wounded, he would be operated on by the battalion doctor. On 15 May, a German Dornier bomber was hit and the crew rowed a dinghy to the other side of the fjord.

When the British Independent Company retreated from Finneid, it was decided to sight them where B Company was located and move B Company to the other side of the fjord to discourage the Germans from approaching from there. On 16 May, the main bridge was blown, though the structure only subsided, making it impassable to vehicles. It could still make a good base for a footbridge. A better job was done that evening on the wooden bridge with axes.

Oberstleutnant Sorko with his II./Gebirgsjager-Regiment 137 and Major Schratz's III./Gebirgsjäger-Regiment 138 were supported by two companies from Gebirgsjäger-Regiment 136 plus a Radfahr-Schwadron

On 16 May, a ski company was formed from elements of 6./Gebirgsjäger-Regiment 137 equipped with SMGs. They had the special mission of getting astride the road to Mo. Here the ski company is seen crossing Korgenfjell. (Arkiv i Nordland, CC BY-SA 2.0)

An abandoned British field fortification made of earth and timber at Stien. Oberstleutnant Sorko was told that strong British defences existed at Stien. He realized a frontal attack would be costly, as the road ran along the shore of the fjord with cliffs and steep slopes on the other side. Hauptmann Vogl-Fernheim's 7. and 8./Gebirgsjäger-Regiment 136 with Sorko's 6. and 8./Gebirgsjäger-Regiment 137 encountered the Scots Guards on 18 May. (Arkiv i Nordland, CC BY-SA 2.0)

The ski platoon of German 6./Gebirgsjäger-Regiment 137 takes a break from toiling through the snow to pose for a group photograph. Early on 17 May, a British plane appeared, forcing the men to hide among the rocks as they departed the tree line. The alpine platoon was dispatched. The slope of the Dalselv was steep and rocky and the men still with the main force had to carry the skis; the ice was cracking and time was lost finding a place that was still frozen enough to get to the other side. The afternoon was no easier with cliffs and snowdrifts to negotiate. At 1600hrs on 17 May, Oberleutnant Gartner could hear the noise of battle. By 1700hrs, Skogan was reached. (Arkiv i Nordland, CC BY-SA 2.0)

from Gebirgsjäger-Regiment 222. At 1000hrs on 16 May, Sorko ordered Oberleutnant Gartner, commander of 6./Gebirgsjäger-Regiment 137, to conduct a march around the Scots Guards' position at Stien, starting late that day, with his ski platoon, accompanied by a specialist Alpine platoon. He departed Finneid and headed for Flogenget, where he would encounter the Dalselv 5km upstream from the fjord. On 17 May, other platoons of German 6./Gebirgsjäger-Regiment 137 started the march with fine sunshine on the road along the Rannenfjord from Finneid to Mo – 26km. Stien, surrounded by mountain heights rising to 900m, could be seen once out of Finneid. The southern slopes rising from the fjord were the locations of the Scots Guards' positions. Heights above 100m were snow-covered. Gartner, with his platoon and the alpine platoon, was told to get astride the road.

A battery of mountain guns was allocated to III./Gebirgsjäger-Regiment 138, pulled along by requisitioned vehicles, to protect against British naval forces firing from the fjord. German 7./Gebirgsjäger-Regiment 137 was at the front on the morning of 17 May, supported by a mortar group and some pioneers. Some 500m from the exploded bridge at Stien, enemy fire was experienced from guns and mortars when they entered an open stretch of road, causing numerous casualties. Sorko ordered the mountain guns forward. He could see the British had made good use of the terrain to conceal positions.

At 1600hrs, the German infantry guns and howitzers were positioned to fire on the rocky slope. Deploying to the open ground would be dangerous. HMGs were sent forward to the lead company and ordered to attack on the wooded slope. Enemy positions were difficult to spot, especially as they were being economical with ammunition. A German reconnaissance aircraft circled above Stien at 1700hrs and was fired upon by the British, showing the Germans the locations of some British guns. Sorko expected the skiers of 6./Gebirgsjäger-Regiment 137 to be in position soon; the expected time for the march was 20 hours. Unfortunately, contact with them was impossible.

The reconnaissance plane could not spot them. Sorko decided to use the rest of 6./Gebirgsjäger-Regiment 137 and 8./Gebirgsjäger-Regiment 137 to conduct a close envelopment. Meanwhile, because British guns and mortars could target the German baggage train, this had to be brought further back. Ammunition was depleted because the Germans were limited to what they could bring along on the sleds. Then Sorko heard the rattle of MG 34s, and by the end of the day he knew Gartner was fighting the British. Gartner reported that they were on the heights above Mo by 2130hrs on 17 May. Norwegian skiers were encountered on the approach. At 1700hrs, the German high alpine group had reached the farmstead near the smelting works and engaged the Norwegians on the final approach. The appearance caused the British leadership some uncertainty. The platoon would be defeated by a Swedish platoon commanded by Captain Bjorkmann when they attacked the road south of Mo.

Soldiers from the Scots Guards march into captivity at Stien. The Germans also captured a good deal of weapons and equipment at Stien. Sorko's force lost 14 dead and 26 wounded. The Scots lost about 70 men. (Arkiv i Nordland, CC BY-SA 2.0)

In the early afternoon of 17 May, the British 25pdrs had started firing, because Germans were seen at Forneset on the road to the front of A Company. Battalion HQ reported to D Company that the Germans had climbed the hills and would attempt to get round the position. At 1700hrs, when German infantry guns and mortars had fired back, A Company was the chief target along with the British Independent Company. HMGs also started to fire. At 1800hrs, a message from Battalion HQ reported that Norwegian patrols had detected 150 Germans on the frozen lake seven miles up the valley. The telephone line then failed. A Norwegian boy also told them that he had spotted the Germans. D Company could then see Germans on an open, snow-covered hill marching in single file and entering some trees. The sun went behind the hill at 2030hrs. The platoon leaders collected some food from Company HQ.

On 18 May, 6./Gebirgsjäger-Regiment 137 led the pursuit of Allied forces following the battle at Stien, with equipment loaded onto carts. Feldwebel Kral, a student about to be promoted to Leutnant, was killed by enemy fire while approaching Mo, along with two others. Apart from this, Mo was occupied without further resistance and 6./Gebirgsjäger-Regiment 137 remained there until 0700hrs on 20 May. (Arkiv i Nordland, CC BY-SA 2.0)

Then, at 2130hrs, 16th Platoon was attacked. Company commander Major Lindsey thought, wrongly, this was by the 150 Germans of the detachment that were making the encircling manoeuvre. 16th Platoon asked for assistance. Lindsey wanted to keep 17th Platoon along the Dalselv and 18th Platoon behind 16th Platoon. He ordered a section from each platoon to help. A runner reported to Company HQ that 16th Platoon had retreated from its positions to behind the HQ hut, because losses were heavy. Company HQ deployed to cover the open area to the front of the hut while the platoon was reorganized. The twilight made aiming difficult and helped the Scots reorganize. Lindsey took five men and stationed them on the hill above Company HQ, as the Germans had already got past 18th Platoon. Lindsey also sent Lieutenant Milburne

Troops from Gebirgsjäger-Regiment 137 rest at the blasted bridge in Selfors, north of Mo. Here, a long wire rope and boats were used to make a ferry. At the next destroyed bridge, *Pioniere* from German 10./Gebirgsjäger-Regiment 137 supported what was left of the structure to make a manageable crossing by 2230hrs. The carts and horses again requisitioned would prove useful and by 0300hrs, Nevernes was reached. (Arkiv i Nordland, CC BY-SA 2.0)

The temporary bridge at Storjord built by German *Pioniere* to replace the destroyed structure. On 23 May, British No. 3 Independent Company took up positions supporting the Scots Guards on high ground near Viskiskoia. British No. 3 Independent Company was thrown off the high ground and the main position was turned. At 1800hrs, Gubbins ordered the Scots Guards' battalion commander, Major Graham, to pull back to Storjord. Force HQ was attempting to make the position at Bodø a base from which to launch counter-attacks. Keeping the Germans at bay from the position at Pothus would allow sufficient time for defences to be built. (Arkiv i Nordland, CC BY-SA 2.0)

to see if A Company could redeploy to counter-attack the Germans that had gone past D Company. With no sign of Milburne and the twilight starting to brighten, Lindsey went to A Company. He reached the position and once he was told where Major Crabbe was, he started up a slope to find him. Then a bullet struck him on his upper right arm. He heard a German utter a shout. He fell back and rolled down the slope for some distance. His pistol had disappeared into the undergrowth.

With Germans infesting the area between the companies, he thought it best to make for Battalion HQ. About 100 yards of open ground needed to be risked, with only a small hollow with some bushes located in the middle offering any hope of staying out of sight. The German who had shot him immediately noticed him when he started his dash. Twice Lindsey felt a bullet pass him before he stumbled into the hollow. He did not stop for long, making another 50-yard dash to the woods, hearing two to three more shots go wide. By accident, he reached Major Crabbe's position and was encouraged to keep to the hillside on his journey to Battalion HQ. Despite this, in full daylight the Germans on the south bank could see him and, from 400 yards, bursts of MG fire were aimed his way until he went around the slope of the hill. He then found himself on a steep slope high above Battalion HQ when a burst of fire landed at his feet. He set off down the slope and not until he reached the road 150–200 yards from Battalion HQ did the hillside hide him from sight. Once at HQ he was told the battalion had ordered a retreat sometime ago. HQ trenches were being targeted and personnel were getting ready to pull out. On the fjord's edge they could not be seen, as they were on the other side of an embankment. About half a mile away, when the shore turned into a cliff, they needed to climb onto the road again, this time out of German sight. Another mile along the road, a truck for wounded

82

personnel stopped and took him on board. He was brought to Bodø and then Harstad, where he was treated.

B Company joined the battalion following a long march on the other side of Ranfjord. The company that had stayed at Bodø was also brought forward. On 19 May, Trappes-Lomax and Gubbins had met near Mo. Trappes-Lomax did not want to wait at Mo for ships to evacuate his battalion as Gubbins wanted, telling Gubbins that ships would be easy targets for aircraft if they had to sail the length of Ranfjord. He stated he wanted to withdraw north of the snow plateau immediately and occupy defences the other side. Then a signal from Force HQ told him he was to stand and fight south of the snow plateau. When Lieutenant-Colonel Dowler from Force HQ met him, Dowler was persuaded that orders could be amended to state he was to conduct a fighting withdrawal. Gubbins then authorized withdrawals if there was serious danger to the force's safety. Trappes-Lomax thought his battalion was already experiencing a precarious situation and decided to use local buses to go over the high, snowy plateau. A German reconnaissance aircraft spotted them and was shot out of the sky by a Bren gunner, so it could not report this subterfuge. When Gubbins heard that the Scots had not delayed the Germans at the plateau, he ordered the Irish Guards with Stockwell's British No. 2 Independent Company forward from Bodø to Pothus. They sailed along Saltdalfjord and then marched on the Saltdalen road to Pothus. Gubbins fired Trappes-Lomax on 23 May, who he blamed for endangering the Storjord positions he was preparing by his precipitous retreat.

A British truck and troops, probably at Mo, during the Allied retreat. On 23 May at 0730hrs, a British lorry carrying engineers and explosives was intercepted on its way to blow up a bridge a few kilometres away. The Germans formed a special section armed with SMGs to capture the bridge by using the lorry as cover, but the subterfuge did not work. The fight was won once the rest of the battalion closed up. (Arkiv i Nordland, CC BY-SA 2.0)

POTHUS, 25–26 MAY 1940

The Irish Guards had departed for Bodø on destroyers and fishing craft on 20 May, and on the 23rd were told that they would assist the Scots Guards. The Saltdalsfjord forms the Saltdalen Valley and was the only practical route north from Mo for the Germans. The Irish Guards, British No. 2 and No. 3 Independent Companies, the 25pdrs of 203 Battery, 51st Royal Artillery Regiment, plus a Norwegian company from II./14th Infantry Regiment, with an HMG platoon and mortar section, were deployed to Pothus. Gubbins kept many of his other formations back to guard against any encircling operation by sea or air. Lieutenant-Colonel Stockwell, the commander of British No. 2 Independent Company, was appointed force commander (Stockforce). Stockwell placed Stockforce on both sides of the Saltdal, guarding a partially destroyed bridge plus a footbridge on a tributary.

Late on 23 May, Stockwell inspected the Pothus position. The road along the banks of the Salt approached Pothus with its bridge at the base of a high ridge. Stockwell thought this strong position could be protected from turning movements by forces stationed on the high ground. A platoon of 55 men from British No. 2 Independent Company and the company's support platoon were positioned on either side of the Salt, on the 23rd, among woods with good lines of sight.

The Irish Guards approached on the morning of 24 May. The 1./Irish Guards was positioned on the high ground south of the bridges near the support platoon, out of communication except by messenger, because signallers could not work the radio sent by Force HQ and there was not enough cable for a telephone line. The intention was to hold as long as possible and then withdraw. A 3./Irish Guards platoon was stationed on the suspension bridge. Engineers had prepared the main girder bridge and the suspension bridge for demolition. The engineer NCO by the main bridge had orders to wait until the Scots Guards had reached the other side and not to detonate without an order from Stockwell. 3./Irish Guards' other platoons defended the tributary from the other side of the Salt. 4./Irish Guards was on a high plateau on the right of the position with good lines of sight to the road. A company from 2nd Norwegian Line Battalion was split between 1. and 4./Irish Guards. An MG platoon, commanded by Captain Ellinger, was also with 1./Irish Guards. A Norwegian mortar section deployed near the Salt Bridge while the 25pdrs were sighted to fire on the main road. British No. 4 Independent Company was at Finneid to cover any withdrawal. 2./Irish Guards was Gubbins' reserve, as was British No. 3 Independent Company, from 2000hrs on 24 May, both located with his HQ by Pothus Wood. The carrier section with the rest of British No. 2 Independent Company would also be positioned there when they arrived.

The sunny day assisted the digging of entrenchments in soft soil. The Scots Guards went through the positions later in the twilight darkness. At 0135hrs on 25 May, the main bridge was blown up; the TNT was detonated by the engineer NCO on orders from a Scots Guards officer. 1./Irish Guards was isolated. At 0800hrs on 25 May the support platoon from stone and log entrenchments spotted a German cycle column on the road. They fired on an open section and most of the Germans were hit. The enemy deployed onto the slopes, and by midday, with permission to pull back, the support platoon was brought to the area near the destroyed bridge; 1./Irish Guards, supported by the Norwegians, was still holding.

By the early afternoon, German infantry of 7./Gebirgsjäger-Regiment 136, supported by five Heinkel bombers, attacked the position. Bombs hit Stockwell's HQ, forcing it to relocate, though he was uninjured. The aircraft raked the wood with machine-gun fire. RSM Stack ordered Battalion HQ onto the road near the eastern edge of the wood in order to race through it when the bombers climbed to turn. The German infantry attack on 1./Irish Guards was thrown back when they rushed onto the ridge throwing grenades, so they decided to go round the company's position. Captain B. Eugster was the commanding officer. By late afternoon he had ordered Lieutenant E. FitzClarence with two platoons to the suspension bridge. Eugster followed with the last platoon. They found the bridge blown and nowhere suitable to get to the other side of the tributary. The Germans soon found the Irish Guards had disappeared and followed. Rifle slings were tied together and Guardsman Murphy with the end was swept 100 yards along the tributary.

The destroyed bridge at Pothus. Stockwell decided this was a good place to stop the Germans. He knew they might deploy forces through the rough wooded ground on the western bank or onto the slopes opposite. A brigade might have stopped them indefinitely. (Arkiv i Nordland, CC BY-SA 2.0)

He got to the other side to tie the end off. Eugster anchored himself on an island to help his soldiers withstand the current. All the while he was being fired at. Laying low, he was not able to join his platoon. By 1900hrs, 1./Irish Guards had withdrawn. The company made it along the path to the footbridge on the Salt. The support platoon, on wooded, hilly positions, was standing firm until 1700hrs when a determined German attack got to within 50 yards. It also was withdrawn.

Meanwhile, 4./Irish Guards was still on the hill holding the Germans on the opposite side of the Salt, despite being subjected to heavy machine-gun and mortar fire. Drummer Hughes of the Intelligence Section and his Norwegian interpreter had set up an observation post near Pothus Bridge. At 1500hrs, when they noticed Germans had used rafts to cross the Salt 800 yards away, they went to the other side of the Salt opposite 4./Irish Guards. Hughes spotted targets for the guns, leading Sorko to build his pontoon further south and await support from Schratz's battalion. Stockwell ordered 2./Irish Guards to the 2,500ft hill on the eastern bank to guard against the Germans using this approach. British No. 3 Independent Company would defend the slope of the height. Both used the track and footbridge and by 0430hrs the next day 2./Irish Guards occupied point 800, the highest peak there.

A German machine gunner with an MG 34 in the Saltdalen Valley, 24 May 1940. (Arkiv i Nordland, CC BY-SA 2.0)

During the darkness, the German *Pioniere* were building a bridge to switch the approach to the opposite bank. Hughes also could see them at work. At 0600hrs he and his Norwegian interpreter noticed two boats. At 0800hrs, an MG with its ammunition was loaded onto them. The pontoon bridge was also being used by Germans who then occupied woods when on the opposite side. By 0900hrs the platoon of British No. 2 Independent Company on this side of the Salt was pushed back. At 0300hrs, the rest of British No. 2 Independent Company had joined Stockwell and he used them to counter this new German attack, holding the enemy back for a time.

That morning Gubbins had been told about the Allies' decision to evacuate Norway. He ordered Stockwell to withdraw to Fauske and prepare to embark at Bodø between 1 and 3 June. At 1600hrs, Stockwell met with 3. and 4./Irish Guards' commanding officers by Pothus Wood and Stockwell told them to withdraw. They only departed at 1800hrs because of the difficulties of being heard above the din of German aircraft. 4./Irish Guards was to start at 1900hrs. British No. 2 Independent Company by the footbridge would cover the Irish Guards' withdrawal until 2230hrs. However, 4./Irish Guards was in close contact with the enemy and could not get away. The appearance of Gloster Gladiators from Bodø machine-gunning the Germans gave the company the chance it needed. They passed Pothus Wood and some Battalion HQ personnel joined them. RSM Stack made sure that the ammunition depot was loaded onto a truck. Stack with 23 men of Battalion HQ went on foot, but they were ambushed on the road and only Stack and another guardsman got away. Drummer Hughes reached Battalion HQ at 2100hrs and used the woods to stay out of sight. He found a section belonging

Note: gridlines are shown at intervals of 1km (0.6 miles).

GERMAN
A. 2.Radfahr-Schwadron
B. Pionier Zug
C. 7./Gebirgsjäger-Regiment 136
D. II./Gebirgsjäger-Regiment 137 (less elements)
E. Zug, Radfahr-Schwadron
F. 6./Gebirgsjäger-Regiment 137
G. III./Gebirgsjäger-Regiment 138 (less elements)

POTHUS

137

SORKO

THE IRISH GUARDS AT POTHUS, 25/26 MAY 1940

Shown here is the British defence of the Saltdalen.

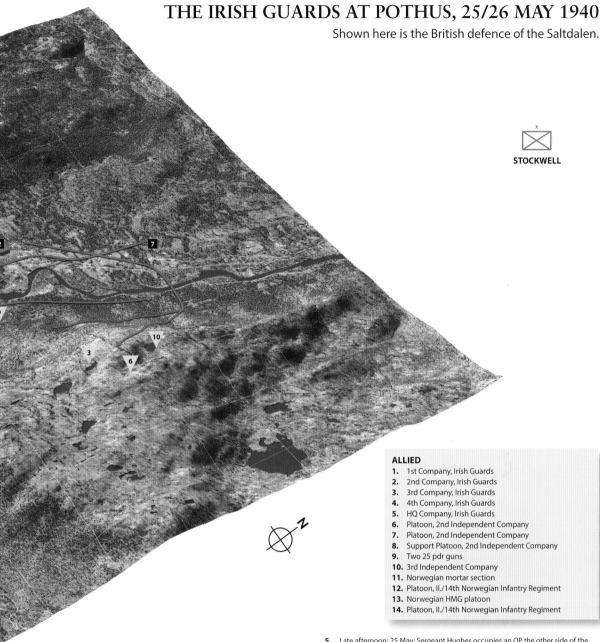

STOCKWELL

ALLIED
1. 1st Company, Irish Guards
2. 2nd Company, Irish Guards
3. 3rd Company, Irish Guards
4. 4th Company, Irish Guards
5. HQ Company, Irish Guards
6. Platoon, 2nd Independent Company
7. Platoon, 2nd Independent Company
8. Support Platoon, 2nd Independent Company
9. Two 25 pdr guns
10. 3rd Independent Company
11. Norwegian mortar section
12. Platoon, II./14th Norwegian Infantry Regiment
13. Norwegian HMG platoon
14. Platoon, II./14th Norwegian Infantry Regiment

▼ EVENTS

1. Morning 25 May: Major Sorko orders 7./Gebirgsjäger-Regiment 136 to lead the assault on the height on the eastern bank when a cycle patrol is fired upon on the road. The attack is thrown back by 1st Company, Irish Guards.

2. Afternoon 25 May: Sorko brings up mortars and HMGs. 7./Gebirgsjäger-Regiment 136 forces Captain Eugster, commanding 1st Company, to withdraw to the suspension bridge. He finds the bridge destroyed. Rifle slings strung together enable the company to gain the opposite side. Eugster with the last platoon is pinned down and unable to join his company at the footbridge.

3. Late afternoon 25 May: Lieutenant-Colonel Stockwell, worried the Germans could dominate his position from height 800, sends 2nd Company, Irish Guards to the position. 3rd Independent Company is ordered to occupy the lower slopes. Both set off early evening.

4. Late afternoon, 25 May: A cycle platoon uses a pontoon raft to get to the other side of the Saltdalen. They exchange fire with 4th Company, Irish Guards.

5. Late afternoon: 25 May: Sergeant Hughes occupies an OP the other side of the destroyed bridge at 1500hrs. He spots German positions for 25-pdr guns and the main bombardment early next morning persuades Sorko to postpone his attack until III./Gebirgsjäger-Regiment 138 reaches him. Also Sorko is persuaded to move the pontoon site further away from the British positions.

6. 0430hrs, 26 May: 2nd Company, Irish Guards is on height 800.

7. Morning, 26 May: Stockwell, with a platoon of 2nd Independent Company, throws back further German forces that used the pontoon ferry and the cyclists.

8. Late afternoon 26 May: Stockwell orders 3rd and 4th companies, Irish Guards to withdraw from positions near the destroyed bridge. III./Gebirgsjäger-Regiment 138 is about to get to the position. At 1900hrs, 4th Company, Irish Guards starts to withdraw.

9. Early evening, 26 May: Hughes with a platoon from 3rd Company, Irish Guards, uses rifle slings strung together to get to the path on the other side of the Salt away from Germans patrolling Pothus Wood.

10. Evening, 26 May: 2nd Company, Irish Guards is told of the British withdrawal by the Norwegian interpreter. 3rd Independent Company has already departed. 2nd Company, Irish Guards starts to withdraw.

Gebirgsjäger Rudi Margreiter of 7./Gebirgsjäger-Regiment 137 in Saltdalen on the east bank of the river at Pothus, 25 May 1940. (Arkiv i Nordland, CC BY-SA 2.0)

to 3./Irish Guards. They were fired on while on open ground near the Salt and used the current to sweep them to safety. Near some boulders, they found a platoon and used rifle slings to get to the opposite bank.

British No. 3 Independent Company on the slope of point 800 was told of the withdrawal by the runner, a Norwegian interpreter, Captain Hartmann; he was supposed to bring the order to 2./Irish Guards on the peak. A sergeant pocketed the message and 2./Irish Guards would be told of the withdrawal five hours later. British No. 3 Independent Company had to retreat along the eastern bank of the Salt to the fjord and did not use the footbridge. 2./Irish Guards only started to follow them when towards the end of the day the Norwegian liaison officer told them that the Germans had occupied Pothus Wood. Eight miles on at Nestby, two miles from the fjord, Stockwell organized a blocking position with two platoons of 4./Irish Guards and the Norwegian MG platoon. There, the stragglers were received.

At the fjord, a Norwegian ferry and ten fishing boats assembled by officers of British No. 2 Independent Company slowly brought most of Stockforce, including British No. 3 Independent Company, to the other side of the fjord. Demolition charges on the quay were about to blow when the ferry, alongside the quay with 350 men on board, caught fire because the engine had worked too hard. The passengers tried to put the fire out by bailing water with buckets and helmets while Lieutenant Fell used his fishing craft to push the ferry off the quay. The ferry got 50–60 yards clear when the charges exploded. The ferry was being towed away when German cyclists appeared, who began to fire on the boats. However, no casualties were suffered. 2./Irish Guards did not get to the quay by the time the last boats sailed and on 27 May had to march 20 miles to Langset on the other side of the fjord, where a requisitioned Norwegian bus from Fauske met them and shuttled them to safety. Meanwhile, at Finneid, British No. 4 Independent Company encountered Stockforce once they had disembarked from the boats. Stockwell deployed most of his companies to a position to cover the approaches to Bodø. He had British No. 1 and No. 3 Independent Companies stay at Finneid. The Germans appeared on the afternoon of 28 May. The evacuation of Irish Guards from Bodø by destroyer, following a 20–25 mile march, started on the morning of the next day. Fishing craft picked up the Independent Companies and brought them to Bodø, where they too would be embarked.

THE ALLIED EVACUATION

The situation at the end of May was not clear. On the 16th, the British force commander had written to the Chiefs of Staff stating that if northern Norway was to be held, he needed 17 battalions, ten cruisers and destroyers, 28 gun batteries and some tanks. On 20 May, with France quickly collapsing,

Churchill argued that forces should be withdrawn from Norway. The distraction of German forces from France that the campaign was supposed to achieve was not happening. Sweden would not agree to an occupation of the ore mines, and had helped with the transit of German supplies through to Narvik. The War Cabinet, with the Chiefs of Staff agreeing, determined on this course of action, following the destruction of the ore facilities. Formal endorsement came on 31 May. Late on the 24th Cork was told to prepare his force to evacuate. He was not to tell the Norwegian government before 1 June. The dangers posed by the German air threat would be stressed to the Norwegians when told of the plan. The Norwegians had suggested the Mowinckel Plan, whereby northern Norway would not be attacked if the Allies withdrew and Swedish forces patrolled the demarcation line. The Germans would not agree to this.

Cork had the cruisers *Southampton* and *Coventry* and about ten destroyers. Late on 3 June, with planes flying from Bardufoss and from the carriers, the first ships sailed. Luckily, the weather was not good and German aircraft stayed away. Fishing craft or destroyers took the men on board the transports. Early on 31 May, the carriers *Ark Royal* and *Glorious* with five destroyers had departed Scapa Flow. *Glorious* was going to embark the Bardufoss aircraft. Some 15 ships and eight transports gathered at different locations 150 miles offshore and would close to the coast by twos, load the men, and gather again to wait at the same points until all had been loaded. Between 4 and 6 June, 14,000 men loaded onto six ships of Group I. On the morning of 7 June, they gathered and headed for Scapa Flow. A battleship from the Home Fleet and escorting destroyers guided them between the Faroes and Shetlands. Eight store ships also departed Harstad on 7 June. The ten Gladiators were flown on board on 7 June. Nine Hurricanes with sandbags attached to the tails also managed a landing. Bardufoss runway was cratered by 120 demolitions. Group II, seven transports, then embarked 5,200 men on 7 June and 4,600 men on the following day. They departed that morning. *Ark Royal* joined them, as did *Southampton* with the HQ staff on board. The Norwegians did not embark. They were pressing on to Bjørnfjell in the expectation of defeating the Germans.

On 26 April, as British naval codes had changed, the Germans did not know the situation off Harstad. On the 25th, the battlecruisers *Scharnhorst* and *Gneisenau*, the Kriegsmarine stated, would soon be able to launch an operation. *Admiral Hipper*, with four to six destroyers, would also be ready. The German staff organized Operation *Juno* to attack shipping at Harstad before a prolonged sortie to the Norwegian Sea. The Germans knew that the British aircraft carriers *Ark Royal* and *Glorious* were somewhere off the coast between Lofoten and Tromsø. On 8 June, *Admiral Hipper* with the destroyers needed fuel and were told to sail to Trondheim. The battlecruisers then sank two merchantmen and thought the position of the German ships had been compromised despite efforts to block signals they had sent. Admiral Marschall, commanding the expedition, was wrong and he perhaps could have risked another fueling at sea operation. Dietl by then knew the Allies were withdrawing and if a communication link had existed between Trondheim's army HQ and Marschall, then he would probably have kept his force united.

At 1546hrs, *Scharnhorst* sighted smoke. That morning *Glorious* had asked permission to steam to Scapa Flow independently. With

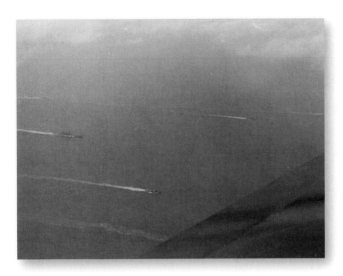

Scharnhorst and destroyers at sea. Flottenchef Admiral Wilhelm Marschall was told to support Dietl by attacking Allied shipping. The German fleet departed on the morning of 4 June. On 6 June, the fleet fuelled from a tanker near Jan Mayen. On 7 June, cloud hampered information gathering on the locations of the British fleet by German aircraft. Marschall needed to know the locations if he was to steam through the fjords, where he could be exposed to shore defences, mines and torpedo batteries. Convoys of ships were detected, though not sailing through the areas in which he was told to operate. He started to think the Allies were evacuating. (Tim Oliver/Alamy)

the two destroyers *Acasta* and *Ardent* accompanying her, *Glorious* started out at 0253hrs at 22 knots. Her captain, G. D'Oyly-Hughes, wanted to get his ship back to Scapa quickly to attend a court martial. He had disagreed with Commander J. Heath about the operations of the aircraft on board. D'Oyly-Hughes had frequently ignored the advice of his senior officers and when Heath objected to sending his Swordfish against ill-defined targets near Mosjøen, the captain had the commander disembark when back at Scapa Flow to await court martial. On 7 June, Bletchley Park had forwarded information that the German naval forces had steamed through the Baltic heading for Norway. However, this information was not acted upon. The Signals Intelligence should have prompted the dispatch of Sunderland flying boats to confirm whether the force was only U-boats, as they suspected.

D'Oyly-Hughes on *Glorious* was told of mastheads sighted 20 minutes after the Germans had spotted the carrier. The British destroyers were only 370m from the carrier, but no aircraft were flying looking out for enemy ships or submarines. A Swordfish was flown to identify the sighting. Another 15–20 minutes elapsed before D'Oyly-Hughes changed course and increased speed. Ten aircraft were operational, though none were on deck. A Swordfish and two Sea Gladiators were at ten minutes' notice, though the Swordfish were not equipped with torpedoes and none were on deck. Admiral Pound would criticize this lack of readiness. At 1627hrs, *Gneisenau* opened fire at 28,000m with the main guns. *Scharnhorst* soon started to fire as well. The first 28cm shells crashed onto *Glorious*' flight deck, destroying the Swordfish about to take off and exploding among the Hurricanes stored below. A fire soon spread and isolated the torpedo store. The fire was brought under control, though the flight deck could not be used and no aircraft could take off.

Once through the smoke screens created by the destroyers, *Glorious* was again visible to the Germans, and the hull was damaged below the waterline. The carrier continued to steam at 20 knots with the battlecruisers closing from 20,000m to 12,500m. *Glorious* could not hide for long and emerged again, to be hit numerous times. The order to abandon ship was piped between 1720hrs and 1730hrs. *Scharnhorst* stopped targeting the ship at 1729hrs. *Gneisenau* stopped soon after. *Glorious* was sinking and the crew jumped from the flight deck and swam towards the carley floats. At 1734hrs, *Scharnhorst* was hit by a torpedo from one of the destroyers on the starboard side by the turret. The magazines caught fire. The starboard engine was out of action. Her speed slowed to 20 knots, though the ship could still manoeuvre and fire back. With 2,500 cubic metres of flooding, Marschall decided to steam to Trondheim without attempting to pick up any of *Glorious*' crew. Signals reporting the attack on *Glorious* were sent on the wrong frequencies and no Allied ships steamed towards the sinking. Both destroyers *Acasta* and *Ardent* were also sunk.

AFTERMATH

The Allied attempt to deny the Germans the Swedish iron ore supplies had failed. Launched when the Swedish ports on the Gulf of Bothnia were about to open again with the spring, its effect was bound to be limited. The Allies needed to hold onto Narvik throughout the summer if they wanted to affect the supply of iron ore from the harbour the following winter. With the campaign to defeat France leading to a rapid German success, British leaders felt they needed to deploy forces back to Britain. With the Luftwaffe about to launch a battle for air supremacy over England, sending enough aircraft to Norway to support a Royal Navy presence at Harstad would be too risky. Radar stations were what made the air defence of Britain credible and possible. Such facilities did not exist at Harstad.

CONCLUSION

Churchill did not make up his mind on whether to concentrate on Trondheim or Narvik. The consequence of this would lead to the British effort being dispersed. Faulty appreciation of intelligence had led to the soldiers being disembarked, with the fleet readied to stop a suspected sortie against the Atlantic shipping lanes. The achievable rapid response to the German landings had a stuttering start. The decision to send the two brigades off quickly embarked to different locations did not help either. The attempted pincer attack on Trondheim with forces landed miles from each other was countered by the Germans when they airlifted reinforcements to Trondheim and marched forces from Oslo. Better to attempt a landing closer and to the north of the city; if a march on Trondheim was blocked then the British force with Norwegian support could still defend the narrow approach to Narvik. The Norwegians could do a good job of pushing back the Germans from positions near Narvik. Then again, the Allies did not think that the Norwegians could defeat the Germans there.

With snow still at the shoreline, the ski-equipped Norwegian soldiers, despite limited training, would always

A solitary Gebirgsjäger looks out over the water at Narvik at the conclusion of the campaign. Sorko's battalion of Gebirgsjäger would stay put and deploy to the border early the following year with 2.Gebirgs-Division to attack the Soviets. They would again be accompanied by the 3.Gebirgs-Division. 2.Gebirgs-Division would fight there for the rest of the war. On the whole, losses were light for 2.Gebirgs-Division marching from the south. Those for 3.Gebirgs-Division were more substantial with III./Gebirgsjäger-Regiment 139 losing 93 killed, 167 wounded and 124 missing. (Arkiv i Nordland, CC BY-SA 2.0)

French soldiers escort a group of Norwegians suspected of spying for the Germans. Mackesy was critical of the support his Norwegian allies could offer, writing to the War Office on 17 April that Norwegian soldiers were almost entirely untrained and that they were utterly untrustworthy, as many helped the Germans. He described Ruge as a crook and Fleischer as a student not a soldier. His criticisms do not stand up. Fleischer's men knew the terrain and conditions, and had the equipment to enable them to operate effectively. (ullstein bild via Getty Images)

OPPOSITE

A Norwegian division commander meets a Gebirgsjäger officer at the surrender of his division. The German opinion of the Norwegian soldier was closer to the mark than Mackesy's. One German officer described them as dangerous opponents, especially when snow cover was apparent, because they were excellent skiers and superb marksmen. If beaten back, they would not hesitate to attack once again on the same ground. (Sueddeutsche Zeitung Photo/Alamy)

be the greatest threat to the Germans. The caution the conditions created among the British senior army officers of 24th (Guards) Brigade stymied any thoughts of using bold tactics. Although they had insufficient landing craft, the huge numbers of Norwegian fishing boats could be used to bring soldiers off the destroyers onto land. With destroyers supporting landings with gunfire, establishing a battalion onshore among the buildings surrounding the harbour was feasible if quickly mounted, following the sinking of the German fleet. By late April, when the bombardment occurred, Dietl was ready to pull out of the town and had started destroying the harbour facilities in the expectation of a British landing.

Mackesy still thought a landing against Narvik was not possible, because his force did not possess landing craft, artillery or enough ammunition for mortars. The rocky shore of the Framnes Peninsula, interspersed with small beaches, was exploited by the Germans, who could set up MG positions among the rocks to fire on the secluded landing grounds. The ground from the beach quickly rose to a crest line the Germans could site reserves beyond; there naval gunfire support with its flat trajectory would be of limited use. Any landing force on the peninsula could be fired on from the other side of the fjord. Mackesy pointed out the wintry conditions his soldiers experienced. Without skis or snowshoes his men could not operate tactically, as thick snow was prevalent even at sea level.

With no landing contemplated, the British 24th (Guards) Brigade was ordered to Bodø to counter a German march north to help Dietl. The evacuation of the British 146th Brigade from Namsos was perhaps not needed. The Namsos force could have used road and rail and, suitably helped by the British Independent Companies, could have delayed the German pursuit if the opinion of the local Norwegian commander had been listened to. The safe deployment of the British 24th (Guards) Brigade once the Germans had established aircraft on Trondheim's runways was bound to be a matter of chance. Hesitancy would not help, neither would the use of large liners. Destroyers could land the battalions and following the *Chorbry* sinking, they were used. If an Allied brigade had been defending the Stien or Pothus position, the Gebirgsjäger would have needed to wait for additional help.

Men of the British 4./Lincolnshire Regiment at Skagge after marching 56 miles across the mountains to escape being cut off by German forces. The British press attaché, Rowland Kenny, noted a tendency to belittle the courage and resisting power of Norwegian soldiers and to emphasize the extent of the treachery of certain Norwegians who favoured the Germans. This he wrote was unworthy, the consequence of a need to find reasons to explain the British military's inability to stop Norway from being captured by the Germans. The British soldiers did not find the Norwegian soldiers a problem. The early losses of military arsenals, combined with poor organization, were the primary causes of Norwegian defeats, not treachery. (© Imperial War Museum, N 82)

German battalion commanders showed they did not want to launch frontal attacks on strongly held British positions. Only because the Allied positions lacked the numbers needed to deploy to defend the whole line could the Germans find weak defences through which to attack the Stien and Pothus positions. The difficulty of attacking through terrain such as steep-sided fjords, widely discussed in doctrinal papers, was not something to be embarked upon lightly. The better choice was perhaps to use the fleet to go around the enemy position, and this was done on occasions with some success. The destruction of the German fleet made such attempts likely to fail, because the British should be able to intercept them.

The Allies could not work out whether the strategic aim was either to help Norway stay fighting Germany or deny the Germans use of the iron ore facilities. If the first, the forces had to land at Trondheim, if the later, at Narvik. The denial of the harbour was not going to be permanent; all that could be done was to destroy the port facilities and railway. This could have been done in a commando-style raid, not in a landing on the scale seen. The force landed by the Allies was intended to march on the Swedish iron ore facilities and included many support personnel. German landings should have ended any thoughts of such an operation and the force balance needed changing, as did the aims of the landing force. Planning modifications on such a large scale at such a late stage would only be possible if the whole purpose of the operation was considered again. This was beyond British decision-making practices.

BIBLIOGRAPHY

Primary sources
Diary of the Earl of Lindsey
Kriegstagebuch, II./Gebirgsjäger-Regiment 137
Kriegstagebuch, 6./Gebirgsjäger-Regiment 137
Kriegstagebuch, Otto Erlacher
II./Gebirgsjäger-Regiment 137 reports, 6 July 1940
Secondary sources
Buchner, Alex, translated Ancker, J.W., *Narvik: The Struggle of Battle Group Dietl in the Spring of 1940*, Oxford, Casemate (2020)
Derry, T.K., *The Campaign in Norway*, London, HMSO (1952)
Fitzgerald, Desmond, *History of the Irish Guards in the Second World War*, Aldershot, Gale and Polden (1949)
Joakimsen, Oddmund, *Narvik 1940: Nazi Germany's First Setback During World War II*, Southern Troms Museum (2010)
Ruef, Karl, *Odyssee einer Gebirgsdivision: die 3. Geb Div. im Einsatz*, Graz, Stocker (1976)

General Władysław Sikorski is shown decorating members of the Polish Independent Highland Brigade following the Norwegian campaign. After the evacuation, the Polish troops disembarked on 14/15 June, and were then sent to St Malo, in northern France, where they fought against the Germans. (agencja FORUM/Alamy)

INDEX

Figures in **bold** refer to illustrations.